RISK TERRAIN RTM MODELING MANUAL

THEORETICAL FRAMEWORK AND TECHNICAL STEPS OF SPATIAL RISK ASSESSMENT

FOR CRIME ANALYSIS

By

Joel M. Caplan, Ph.D.

Leslie W. Kennedy, Ph.D.

RUTGERS
Center on
Public
Security

Newark, NJ

This entire book is available to anyone for download at www.riskterrainmodeling.com

Suggested Citation:

Caplan, J. M. & Kennedy, L. W. (2010). *Risk Terrain Modeling Manual.* Newark, NJ: Rutgers Center on Public Security.

Produced by Rutgers Center on Public Security:

Based at the Rutgers University School of Criminal Justice, the Rutgers Center on Public Security (RCPS) offers a multidisciplinary approach to the academic study and practical application of ways in which democratic societies can effectively address crime, terrorism and other threats to public security. This involves the prevention of, protection from and response to natural or human-made events that could endanger the safety or security of people or property in a given area. RCPS engages in innovative data analysis and information dissemination, including the use of GIS, for strategic decision-making and tactical action. Visit RCPS online for current research projects, reports and publications: www.rutgerscps.org

Acknowledgements

All U.S. Census Bureau materials, regardless of the media, are entirely in the public domain. There are no user fees, site licenses or any special agreements, etc., for the public or private use, and/or reuse of any census title. As a tax funded product, it is all in the public record.

Irvington, New Jersey data was provided by the NJ State Police through the Regional Operations Intelligence Center and the many datasets they maintain, validate, and update regularly to support internal crime analysis and police investigations.

Table of Contents

Preface 7

Part 1: Introduction to the Risk Terrain Modeling Approach to Spatial Risk Assessment 9

Chapter One: Theoretical Framework of Risk Terrain Modeling 10
The Concentration of Crime 10
Near Repeats 14
Risk-Based Intelligence-Led Policing 15
Chapter Two: Risk Terrain Modeling Overview and Origin 22
Risk, Terrain, and Modeling 22
Risk Terrain Modeling and Crime Hotspots 27
Forecast Crime Places Better than Retrospective Hotspot Maps 28
Testing the Cohesiveness of Risk Terrain High-risk Cells 33
Using Both RTM and Hotspot Mapping for Police Operations 36

Part 2: Steps and Techniques of Risk Terrain Modeling 40

Chapter Three: A Basic Stepwise Example of Risk Terrain Modeling
(with Screen Captures) 41
Chapter Four: Getting Started with RTM 64
Introduction 64
What You Need to Begin 64
Chapter Five: Steps of Risk Terrain Modeling 71
A Really Brief Overview of the Steps of RTM 71
Detailed Steps of Risk Terrain Modeling 71
Chapter Six: Testing the Statistical Validity of Your Risk Terrain
Model 99

Part 3: Concluding Comments and Caveats 106

Chapter Seven: Risk Terrain Maps as Spatial Intelligence 107
Risk Reduction vs. Response to Crisis 107
Risk Terrain Modeling in ACTION 109

Endnotes 120

Start Here
For a Complete Understanding of RTM

Start Here
To Make Maps Right Away, Then Read Part 1

Preface

Risk is a continuous dynamic value that increases or decreases intensity and clusters or dissipates in different places over time. Valuations of risk are tied to geography and, regarding crime, which occurs at a finite place, risk values are the measure of a place's potential for a crime event to occur. Geographic, or place-based, risk is determined by a nexus of certain factors and changes as the characteristics and interactions of those factors vary. Sometimes all risk factors must interact at the same place and time for the event to occur. Drawing from an example in meteorology, individual factors that are incorporated into weather forecasting do not necessarily produce rain, thunder storms or hurricanes by themselves. It is only when they intersect in space and time that they have the greatest potential to yield a particular outcome, e.g. a storm. Other times, only one or a few factors may be required to interact in the same geography and at certain times for a particular event to occur.

Understanding the spatial-temporal interaction effects of certain factors, or correlates, of crime is key to assessing and valuing criminogenic risk. Fortunately, decades of criminological research have identified a variety of independent variables that have been found to correlate significantly with particular crime outcomes. Risk Terrain Modeling (RTM) was developed by Joel M. Caplan and Leslie W. Kennedy at Rutgers University School of Criminal Justice in recognition that a method was needed to simultaneously apply all of these empirical findings to practice. The intent of RTM is to return to the principle that we can understand crime not just on the basis of knowing what occurred prior to the incident that we are interested in but also that we understand the social and physical contexts in which crime can occur. This approach is consistent with efforts over the years to examine crime in terms of events, that is, to consider the temporal as well as spatial factors that precede, interact with, and follow the incident's occurrence.

Using the "criminal event perspective"[1] as a model of analysis, in this manual we piece together the elements that relate to particular outcomes and consider them as contributing factors to the ways in which crimes emerge and transpire. Importantly, we have operationalized this conceptual framework in a way that can be used to study crime origins, evolution, and impacts on offenders, victims, and environments using state of the art data, analytical tools, and visualization. We acknowledge that the information produced from these efforts needs to be meaningful to law enforcement practitioners. So it is through the development of RTM, which incorporates all of these concepts through a series of tasks, that we hope to make this approach easily accessible to crime analysts and decision-makers at all levels.

This manual is offered as a primer on risk in the criminal event and demonstrates effective ways to apply GIS techniques to data. Through this process, analysts can identify risk terrains that give actionable meaning to the relationships that exist between place-based indicators and crime outcomes. Planners can use this approach to develop strategic models to forecast where crime problems are likely to emerge and to engage in steps that might reduce risks of crime occurring in the future.

The manual is presented in three parts. We begin with a review of the risk terrain modeling approach and present a short overview of the theoretical underpinnings of criminological theory that have addressed the social and environmental factors that contribute to crime patterns, hotspots, and risk terrains. The second part shows an example of the RTM approach and details the technical steps for analysts to take in using ArcGIS software to develop risk terrain maps. In the third and final part, we present ideas of how we see RTM working in strategic and tactical decision-making using the ACTION model developed by Kennedy and Van Brunschot[2].

Introduction to the

Risk Terrain Modeling Approach to

Spatial Risk Assessment

CHAPTER ONE
THEORETICAL FRAMEWORK OF RISK TERRAIN MODELING

The Concentration of Crime

That crime concentrates in specific, select areas, or "hotspots" is well supported by research[3] and comports with the daily experiences of crime analysts in law enforcement agencies across the nation. The identification of crime hotspots tells us where behavior is clustered. Connecting this to precursory environmental context is more challenging but efforts to forecast future crime locations need to address this issue. As Abbott[4] states, "the Chicago School thought that no social fact makes any sense abstracted from its context in social (and often geographic) space and social time. ...Every social fact is situated, surrounded by other contextual facts and brought into being by a process relating it to past contexts" (p. 1152). Ecologists ranging from Burgess and Park to Shaw and McKay sought out ways in which they could extract social indexes from data on communities to use in their explanations of the occurrence and distribution of crime.

Later theorists applied social area analysis to the task of assigning social attributes to urban areas that would describe their propensity to disorganization, disorder and crime[5]. The thread of this work was lost with the increased focus on individual criminality that occurred in the 1960s. But critics warned about losing the focus on social areas. Abbott, for example, derided the efforts in contemporary urban studies to look for single causal factors. To him, the importance of the ecological approach was in its accounting of social interactions that occur in context (an empirical fact that was difficult to test, given the data and technology available at the time, but is now possible with modern analysis packages and better data). Notwithstanding Abbott's warning, the ecologists' views were supplanted, to some degree, with the work of opportunity theorists who looked more at the proximate causes of crime than the contextual ones. This new approach was not completely divorced from the ecological traditions, just more narrowly focused on the transactions between victims and offenders.

Opportunity theorists have suggested that variations in crime are explained by opportunities to commit crime at locations that are accessible to the offender. Cohen, Kluegel, and Land[6] refashioned routine activities theory, that emphasized the co-presence of offenders, victims and guardians, renaming it "opportunity" theory, to include concepts of exposure, proximity, guardianship, and target attractiveness as variables that increase the risk of victimization. But opportunity theorists have yet to agree on a metric for operationalizing "opportunity". A common thread among opportunity theorists and related scholarly thinkers is that the unit of analysis for "opportunity" is a place, and that the dynamic nature of that place constitutes opportunities for crime. For example, Eck[7], Mears, Scott, and Bhati[8], and Brantingham and Brantingham[9] all directly state or imply the place-based nature of criminogenic opportunities. Crime control and prevention activities, then, must consider not only who is involved in the criminal events, "but also the nature of the environments in which these activities take place"[10] (p. 129).

Common to many of these studies[11] is the view that opportunities for crime are not equally distributed across locations[12]. In addressing this, Paul and Patricia Brantingham[13] provided important conceptual tools for understanding relationships between space and crime. They referred to the "environmental backcloth" that emerges from the confluence of routine activities and physical structures overlaying urban areas.

The Brantinghams[14] suggest that this backcloth is dynamic and, importantly, can be influenced by the forces of "crime attractors" and "crime generators"—both of which contribute to the existence of hotspots. Attractors are those specific things that attract offenders to places in order to commit crime. Generators refer to the greater opportunities for crime that emerge from the collection of more people into areas simply as a result of the increased volume of interaction taking place in these areas. Drug markets provide an example of how crime both concentrates at certain places but also evolves in a way that sustains risky places and promotes violent behavior, acting as both attractors and generators of illegal activity[15]. The clustering of such activity in particular areas is supported by the unique combination of certain factors that make these places opportune locations for crime occurrence[16]; that is, where the potential for, or risk of, crime comes as a result of all the characteristics found at these places.

As an attribute of these risk terrains, opportunity is not an absolute value, a dichotomous variable, or a static quotient. It is rarely or never zero. Opportunity varies in degrees and changes over time as public perceptions about environments evolve; as new crimes occur; as police intervene; or as motivated offenders and suitable targets travel. Assessing spatial criminogenic opportunity requires a conceptual framework that is attuned to incorporating multiple dynamic factors and producing intelligence that serves strategic decision-making and tactical responsive action. Risk assessment—"a consideration of the probabilities of particular outcomes"[17] (p.4)—serves this purpose. Considering criminogenic opportunity as place-based risk makes theoretical and intuitive sense to all participants: offenders and victims know they take risks and that these risks increase in certain locations; police consider risks in doing their jobs; and they are often deployed to certain geographies to combat crime and manage other real or perceived threats[18].

A recently revived interest in community analysis brought some of these ideas about place-based risk back into scholarly discussions but without the application of geographic information systems (GIS). Criminologists (among others, including public health, etc.) began talking about crime (i.e. behavior) hotspots, but with few exceptions[19] ignored clusters of the correlates of crime (although see the literature on social disorganization by Sampson, Raudenbush, and Earls[20]). Recent work is beginning to look at the links to risk terrains. Groff[21], for example, has examined the changing character of robberies using an agent based model that accounts for changes over time and for concentration effects. Groff points out that despite its emphasis on the changing character of crime opportunities because of the shifts in routine activities, there has not been a concerted effort in the research literature to actually operationalize this shift, both in temporal and spatial terms. In her test of routine activities, she suggested using a simulation model that assesses the importance of time away from the home, concentration effects of robbery, and physical landscape of the city. In her model, Groff showed that there are definite tendencies for crime to concentrate (as shown in much of the crime hotspots literature) but also to congregate in certain areas according to the structure of the underlying street patterns in the study areas. This is a particularly interesting observation, as it provides support for the notion that physical structure, as well as activity in public, will have an effect on the ways in which crime occurs. While this seems to be a fairly obvious finding, and one that has been imbedded in the research literature for some time, because of data problems and the complexity of the issue, it has been difficult to show empirically how this connection works. Risk terrain modeling addresses this difficulty.

Near Repeats

Another way of considering crime predictors would be to imagine that crime that occurred once might occur again as a result of the previous crime, suggesting a contagion effect. As an extension of, or companion to, hotspot analysis, this approach has been labeled "near repeats"[22]. Analysts have suggested, for example, that we can improve our understanding of the likelihood of terrorism incidents if we have a better handle on "precursor crimes," such as identity theft. The second way of looking at precursors is to see them as creating conditions under which crimes are more likely to occur. For example, if an area is socially disorganized, it may be more likely to attract drug activity which, in turn, may lead to violence. Risk terrain modeling focuses on the second interpretation of precursors but does not preclude the importance of understanding behavioral preconditions to crime that are captured in ideas, such as, near repeats.

Victimization theory talks about this when it refers to repeat victimization. Ratcliffe and Rengert[23], for example, report that in studies of burglary in Philadelphia there were elevated patterns of near-repeat shootings within two weeks and one city block of previous incidents. Further, during this time period, the elevated risk of a shooting was 33 percent greater than expected. This is consistent, the authors said, with the findings of Johnson and Bowers, that suggested proximity in time and space increased the likelihood that crime will repeat[24] and indicates that a complicated set of interactions can lead to the repeat occurrence of crime in certain proximate locations, including retaliation, coercion, and escalation of disputes. It is as though crime occurs in the context of a scripted set of conflicts that emerge out of contested interactions[25]. While it makes sense that social interaction can sustain criminal behavior, the question remains whether or not (and why) there is a contagion effect that promotes a set of re-victimizations in close proximity and soon after the original offense occurs.

The investigations of near repeats provide an important extension of hotspot analysis as it allows for a more dynamic approach that takes into account the temporal link between events and does not just assume that behavior that takes place in close proximity (hotspots) at whatever time in a set frame (a month, a year) has anything to do with other behavior located nearby. But, near repeats also is restricted to the view that re-offending or re-victimization is event dependent. As a forecasting tool, it provides immediate evidence for future behavior but it relies on the occurrence of crime as a foundation for predicting future behavior. Problems that emerge from this approach include the difficulty of accounting for successful law enforcement intervention or steps taken to enhance situational prevention which may successfully reduce recurrence. This result would make new predictions inaccurate, if not impossible. Risk terrain modeling does suffer from this dilemma.

Risk-Based Intelligence-Led Policing

Intelligence-led policing has become the central paradigm for police agencies seeking to incorporate information from advanced sources into decision-making. Intelligence-led policing suggests that a well-informed police agency will perform in a more effective and efficient way. But, the information or intelligence that is communicated to police managers and line officers must be credible, meaningful, and actionable. It must make sense within the context of their jurisdictions and the organizations of which they are a part. In finding a way to implement this paradigm, criminal justice practitioners and police scholars are examining the merits of looking at policing from the point of view of risk, in a manner suggested above, taking the frameworks used in applying information to decision-making through a process of evaluation and priority setting. In this process policing takes on a proactive, strategic direction that reduces the need to be mostly reactive. In addition, the risk approach draws attention to the hazards and dangers that appear both in the communities that are policed but also in the ways in which the policing is done. Through the combined efforts of risk assessment and risk governance, police leaders and police officers are afforded a more systematic approach to enforcing laws and maintaining peace and order in their environments.

Intelligence is a constant process of data collection, analysis, distribution, and assessment. Ratcliffe explained the implementation of the intelligence model in policing as "…the application of criminal intelligence analysis as an objective decision-making tool in order to facilitate crime reduction and prevention through effective policing strategies and external partnership projects drawn from an evidential base"[26] (p.3). Accordingly, three components contribute to this form of policing and, ultimately, crime prevention[27]: the interpretation of intelligence; the influence that this has on decision-makers; and the ultimate impact that this has on the criminal environment. If the intelligence is simply used as a reactive tool, confirming decisions that have already been made and resource allocations already locked in, its usefulness is limited. If intelligence is applied to prospective decision-making, where strategic and tactical decisions are made on the basis of anticipated demands and priorities, the efficacy of the information is greatly enhanced.

The application of a risk-based approach to intelligence-led policing has already begun in the United Kingdom. The National Intelligence Model standardizes police reporting, analysis, and intelligence-based actions in ways that have direct impacts on day-to-day police operations. As John and Maguire[28] observe, the national intelligence model is designed to allow police leadership to move beyond a focus on specific crimes to a more strategic, risk-based approach in identifying areas of concern and developing resource allocation strategies. The intelligence generated by crime analysts, police officers on the street, and targeted surveillance can be combined into a risk assessment that helps set future police action[29]. Despite this observation, policing scholars have been slow on the uptake related to risk-based approaches and there has been limited attention paid to its relevance for intelligence-led policing. Part of the reason for this may be the lack of a comprehensive review of the role of risk in police decision-making. This may derive from concerns that emerge about the problems that risk assessment may generate in the legal and/or ethical use of data in police planning and investigations.

Maguire[30] points out that police researchers have been keenly aware of the ethical dangers in using intelligence in active risk management, including concerns about privacy and control of invasive practices. This danger is further enhanced as risk-based intelligence, unlike general surveillance, targets particular individuals and groups. In this form, it can represent an aggressive form of information collection and decision-making processes, tying up large amounts of police resources[31], and teetering on violations of civil rights. These problems have created some implementation difficulties of the UK national model and Maguire points out that the application has not been widely successful. Nonetheless, the promise of greater accountability and the usefulness in prioritization of policing programs has provided sustenance to a risk-based approach[32].

The allure of risk-based policing is that risk assessment can tie information closely to both strategic and tactical decision-making and provide a means by which police leadership can evaluate interventions and plan future actions. It comports with the idea that the public has anxieties that translate into demands for prevention strategies to reduce crime risk (and fears of crime) and it addresses the idea that certain areas can be more dangerous than others and, therefore, demand greater police attention.

It articulates an evaluation plan that can be used to determine the effectiveness of programs and the efficacy (or waste) of certain types of resources used. It also begins to offer a method of standardizing these decisions in a way that can transfer across jurisdictions. So, risk assessment and risk governance can provide an attractive framework for policing that takes advantage of the sophistication of modern technology and new information from many sources. This framework can also involve more police personnel in dialogues with the public about safety and security issues.

In simple terms, risk is a calculation, based on values, choices, information and perspectives of the likelihood of harm or benefit. This calculation of harm or benefit takes into consideration the types of hazards faced, along with the resources available to diminish the likelihood of harm that hazards pose. At the same time, the calculations of harms and benefits depend upon the temporal stage of the hazardous event (i.e. precursor, transaction, aftermath). Security, therefore, requires equilibrium among the hazards themselves, the resources available to mitigate various hazards, and the stage of the hazardous event[33]. Security may result when hazards are balanced with mitigating resources, yet the balance changes depending on the temporal phase of (exposure to) the hazard. For example, security precursory to the event of a house fire comes from having smoke alarms, fire extinguishers, sprinkler systems, and escape ladders. But, security during and immediately after a house fire comes from 911 dispatchers, firefighters, support from family/friends, and temporary shelter.

Addressing crime from the point of view of risk balance conforms to the ways in which motivated offenders, potential victims, and everyone else talks about confronting dangers and is increasingly becoming the way in which public safety agencies discuss their responses to dangers. Insurance agents to police chiefs, for example, routinely balance what resources they have with what is defined as hazardous at any given moment. Over time and at different stages of an event the balance can change, either because of prevention measures taken prior to an incident, reduced exposure during an incident, or prevention measures that are developed in learning from previous incidents. Across hazards, these balance calculations can vary greatly, with different resources and interventions developed according to the type of hazard, but also according to the stage of the event. The implication of this model is that some or all of these hazards may combine to affect overall exposure to harm and influence the risk balance calculation that may characterize any particular and all realms.

A final point related to the dynamic aspect of security has to do with respective positioning relative to the identified hazard. Whether at the individual or institutional level, danger or potential harm may be perceived as ranging from very likely to very unlikely. For example, we may recognize that school shootings are a possibility, now that we have collectively witnessed such an event, but we may still understand the likelihood of such events as remote. Perceiving a particular threat as either very remote or very likely, as well as being able to imagine the extent of the harm that can be done, will influence the level of preparedness undertaken in advance of such an event. Perceived likelihood therefore varies depending both upon one's temporal and spatial proximity to the hazard itself.

The motivation for police to become "knowledge brokers" of risk should be due in part to the recognition that relevant information that helps to reduce crime comes from a variety of sources, including the community. In their efforts to enhance the cost-effectiveness of the information they collect, police organizations "should be structured to collect, analyze and interpret information from a range of sources, construct it as intelligence and use this to inform how, when, why and against whom they take action" [34]. The idea behind risk-based intelligence-led policing and the increasing rationality of the investigative process is that, rather than policing being an ad-hoc and intuitive enterprise, greater objectivity and rationality are sought to counter these difficulties. Following from the analysis of risk, it is assumed that there would be plans made for intervention, prevention, and mitigation but this cannot be done without an evaluation strategy that provides information, not on the risk this time, but on the effect that the programs have on their intended targets (points we will return to in Part 3 of this manual). This information can feed back through the intelligence cycle. It can also be used to help redesign aspects of the organization in creating more effective delivery and programmatic outcomes.

Finally, the risk process relies on notifying others about the success of the programs that it promotes to mitigate risk. It is also important that the organization is aware of and communicates to others future threats and the limitations that may have emerged in the application of prevention strategies. This is a key element in encouraging the development of innovation within the police agency—using risk assessment as a vehicle for promoting proactive programming and the integration of information and intelligence into police operations.

So, together, the risk environment and the risk organization can be combined to form an information package that can be assessed in terms of risk. The intelligence that is gleaned from this process involves the calculation of harm done if action is not taken to address certain hazards, both in the community and within the police organization. Thinking about the application of intelligence in this way provides a way of examining the negative aspects of hazards, the reputation and integrity risks to the organization, and the temptations to overextend police response to areas that do not warrant action. Chapter 2 begins by discussing the overview and origin of risk terrain modeling as an approach to place-based risk assessment. We then set the discussion of risk based policing in the police paradigms that have developed to date to guide police strategies and tactics. While we will argue that risk terrain modeling is novel in its applications and benefits from the new innovations in information technology and decision-making, it emerges out of a long-standing approach to managing risks in policing.

CHAPTER TWO
RISK TERRAIN MODELING OVERVIEW AND ORIGIN

Risk, Terrain, and Modeling

Crime explanations can be accounted for by different factors that tie different components of risk together to explain individual, group, and institutional influences and impacts on crime events. The criminal event perspective[35] reminds us to anticipate the effects of motivation, vulnerability, and prevention on crime. What is left implicit, and what we make explicit using the concept of risk, is the likelihood of an event beginning, continuing, and ending in a certain way. Risk suggests the likelihood of an event occurring given what is known about the correlates of that event and it can be quantified with positive, negative, low or high ordinal values.

Using risk as a metric, it is possible to model how risk evolves spatially and temporally, accounting for the different stages of the crime event. Modeling broadly refers to the abstraction of the real world at certain places. Specifically within the context of risk terrain modeling (RTM), modeling refers to the acts of attributing the presence, absence, or intensity of qualities of the real world to places within a terrain, and combining multiple terrains together using map algebra[36] to produce a single composite map where the newly derived value of each place represents the aggregated— synthesized or collinear—qualities of those places irrespective of all other places within the terrain. A terrain is a grid of the study area made up of equally sized cells that represent a continuous surface of places where values of risk exist. Raster data is used to represent terrains in RTM. Places are defined by cells of size x^2 (e.g. 100ftx100ft).

Risk terrain modeling[37], then, is an approach to risk assessment that standardizes risk factors to common geographic units over a continuous surface. Separate map layers representing the presence, absence, or intensity of each risk factor at every place throughout a terrain is created in a geographic information system (GIS), and then all map layers are combined to produce a composite "risk terrain" map with attribute values that account for all risk factors at every place throughout the geography. Risk terrain maps assist in strategic decision-making and tactical action by showing where conditions are ideal for events to occur in the future.

Risk terrain modeling operates in a way similar to conventional offender-based risk assessment established many decades ago as research showed that the characteristics of offenders were correlated with their subsequent behavior[38]: offender characteristics are scored and combined to form a scale that is indicative of "risk"—including the risk of re-arrest or reconviction, the risk of jumping bail, or the risk of parole or probation violation[39]. These methods do not reliably predict who will and who will not offend but instead are concerned with the classification of offenders into higher and lower risk groups for the purposes of allocating appropriate criminal justice interventions and resources[40]. RTM is consistent with this tradition except it combines actuarial risk prediction with environmental criminology to assign risk values to places according to their particular attributes.

The technical approach to RTM is straightforward (see, especially, Part 2 of this manual): identify, through meta-analysis or other empirical methods, literature review, professional experience, and practitioner knowledge all factors that are related to a particular outcome for which risk is being assessed[41]. Then, connect each factor to a common geography. Essentially, RTM assigns a (weighted or un-weighted) value signifying the presence, absence or intensity of each risk factor at every place throughout a given location. Each factor is represented by a separate terrain (risk map layer) of the same geography. When all map layers are combined in a GIS, they produce a composite map—a risk terrain map—where every place throughout the geography is assigned a composite risk value that accounts for all factors associated with the particular crime outcome. The higher the risk value the greater the likelihood of a crime event occurring at that location. Risk terrain modeling of crimes produces maps that show places with the greatest risk or likelihood of becoming spots for crime to occur in the future[42], not just because police statistics show that reported crimes occurred there yesterday, but because the social and environmental conditions are ripe for crime to occur there tomorrow.

Risk terrain modeling assumes a step that is basic to the development of geographic information systems in assuming that certain places can acquire attributes that, when combined in prescribed ways, create contexts in which certain outcomes are made more likely. A risk terrain map provides a composite picture of the underlying micro-level conditions throughout a neighborhood, community, city or region. The ways in which these conditions combine is an important aspect for setting up the "meaning" that a risk terrain model will carry. The setting (or terrain) is not static but it is recognizable and sustainable. Its characteristics emerge over time and connect the structure of environment to the activities that occur at these locations. For example, the combined attributes of open space, presence of children, and proximity to schools may indicate a playground. These attributes combined can be used to anticipate the types of behavior that we would expect in a playground, reducing the uncertainty in our forecasts about what would transpire there. In this way, environmental attributes are used as a means of assigning risk (or likelihood) that certain events will happen at a particular place.

These events may be benign (e.g. children playing) or they may take on a more sinister character where a combination of certain types of factors creates a context in which the risk of crime (or other hazardous events) can occur. The advantage of RTM is that it provides a picture of a landscape in terms of factors that contribute to negative events, such as crime, that are more enduring than just the characteristics of the people who frequent these places. This observation about enduring characteristics resonates with the work done by human ecologists (e.g. Shaw and McKay) who set out to construct what they called natural areas, locations that had certain characteristics that led to expected behavioral outcomes, regardless of the character of the people living in or passing through those areas. It also parallels work that has been done on the differentiation between "space" (which connotes only location) and "place" and suggests that location ties to behavior in a predictable, meaningful way. Risk terrain modeling suggests the formation of places that are more malleable than those the ecologists saw in natural areas, but they share the characteristic that they are not pre-defined by the attributes of the people who live or travel there.

RTM considers criminal behaviors as less deterministic and more a function of a dynamic interaction that occurs at places. Place-based attributes are not necessarily constant over time, but the ways in which they interact can be studied to reveal consistent patterns of interaction. The computation of these patterns is a key component of RTM, with the ability to weight the relative importance of different factors at different places and how they influence behaviors and events. The attributes themselves do not create crime; they simply point to locations where, if the conditions are right, the risk of crime or victimization will go up. This might be influenced by factors outside of the context that we are studying, such as the general level of social control that exists across places. But, this, too, can be added as an attribute to be considered in a risk terrain model.

We cannot simply assume, though, that because a location is high in risk according to a risk terrain model that crime will always ensue (any more than we can assume that a location that is a high risk for disease will experience an outbreak, as a matter of course). Important in considering place-based risk is the extent to which we are likely to find that these locations are susceptible or exposed to conditions that promote and/or enable criminal behavior. In the long-standing debate in criminology concerning what promotes crime, it is not really enough to say that risk of crime increases when the number of criminals increase. What is more likely is that the risk of crime at places that have criminogenic attributes is higher than other places because these locations attract motivated offenders (or more likely concentrate them in close locations) and are conducive to allowing certain events to occur. This is different from saying that crime concentrates at highly dense hotspots. It suggests, instead, that individuals at greater risk to committing crime will congregate at locations that are best suited for perpetrating it (i.e. risky locations, from the potential victim's or police perspective). Oddly enough, this is not to say that there are more or better targets[43] of crime (as there may be less to steal and fewer rewards from robbing individuals), but rather that the conditions for criminal behavior (e.g., lower risk of apprehension or retaliation) are better in these places than in others.

Risk terrain modeling is an approach to risk assessment that standardizes risk factors to common geographic units over a continuous surface.

Risk Terrain Modeling and Crime Hotspots

The identification of crime hotspots through mapping, and the targeting of police activity to these places, has been recognized in high-quality evaluation research as an effective crime-fighting technique[44]. Despite the evident success of this technology in operational policing, there is a manifest disconnect between the conventional practice of mapping and the demands by police agencies to be responsive to the dynamic nature and needs of the communities they serve. Crime mapping tends to be restricted to fairly simple density maps based on the retrospective analysis of crime data[45]. This reactive approach makes analysts less attuned to the idea of crime risk or potential and it essentially assumes that crime will most likely always occur precisely where it did in the past—even if police intervene[46]. Among other things, this poses what Brantingham and Brantingham[47] referred to as the "stationarity fallacy" that emphasizes the fact that hotspots are combinations of unrelated incidents that occur over time and are plotted in hotspots as though they are somehow connected beyond sharing a common geography.

Commonsense suggests that hotspot mapping is a reasonable method and research confirms its predictive power[48]. However, research also indicates that the predictive efficacy of mapping can be improved over conventional approaches[49] using multivariate methods[50], raster data[51] and diverse techniques such as RTM, which builds in part on the theoretical insights already reviewed that seek to explain the clustering of crime. The identification of risky areas should permit police to intervene and allocate resources to reduce risk without analysts having to fear the positive impact of intelligence-led interventions. Paradoxically, too much success will avert negative events to the point that crime counts will be reduced and there are none or too few past crimes to be used in traditional inferential statistical forecasting models[52]. This is a problem that emerges from the past crime hotspot approach. In real-world settings, as locations evolve and as police respond to problems in them, crime patterns also change. Risk terrain modeling does not suffer the fate of other techniques that could (and should) put themselves out-of-business if their information products are valid, reliable, and can be easily applied to policing operations.

Forecast Crime Places Better than Retrospective Hotspot Maps

Forecasting approaches undertaken to-date are diverse, some more explicitly embracing theory than others and some relying on more complex statistical techniques. From our point of view, an important consideration for the development of forecasting models is the replicability of the approach by crime analysts using existing and common GIS tools. Also, it should enhance their ability to inform strategic decision-making and operational policing. To be clear, forecasting (i.e. risk assessment) is not the same as predicting. Building on a point made earlier, forecasting is more advantageous to practitioners because it does not rely on a crime to actually occur. Predictions are deterministic in that an event is assumed to happen unless proper actions are taken; any occurrence of the predicted event connotes a failure of the public safety practitioners who were tasked with prevention, while any absence of the predicted event connotes either an adequate practitioner response or a failed predictive model. Unfortunately, the only true measure of success of a predictive model is for the event to occur, which is generally not in the public's or responsible practitioner's best interest. This is why most public safety responses are measured as failures when hazardous events occur or when crises cannot be properly managed. Prevention activities performed in response to predictions always have the burden of proving that those activities were the direct result of the non-event—while assuming that the event would absolutely have occurred otherwise.

While prediction methods focus on the presence or absence of an event, risk assessments using RTM focus on the dynamic conditions of the environment where a crime could occur. The unit of analysis is the geography, not the event. As a case in point, a particular geography's risk of a crime occurring there will be high when conditions at that location are ideal for a crime to occur. The identification of risky areas permits public safety practitioners to intervene and allocate resources to reduce risk at the unit of analysis that they are operationally conditioned for—the geography. The impact of interventions to reduce risk (and avert negative events) can be evaluated by regularly re-assessing risk and then measuring changes in risk values among different risk terrain maps at micro or macro levels either visually or using basic inferential statistics. For example, when evaluating the impact of a police intervention that was taken in response to an assessed risk, subsequent risk terrain maps might be expected to show certain results, such as an overall reduction in risk values throughout the intervention area; a fragmentation or shift of high-risk clusters; or, an equalization of risk throughout the study area—with a decreased intensity of high-risk clusters and a slightly increased or constant intensity of risk at cooler spots (See Figure 1). In this way, the risk assessment model and the interventions performed by public safety practitioners to reduce risk can be appropriately and mutually exclusively credited with success or failure.

The unit of analysis is the geography, not the event.

Risk terrain modeling does not suffer the fate of other techniques that could (and should) put themselves out-of-business if their information products are valid, reliable, and can be easily applied to policing operations to reduce crime.

Figure 1: Risk Terrain Modeling → Action → Evaluation

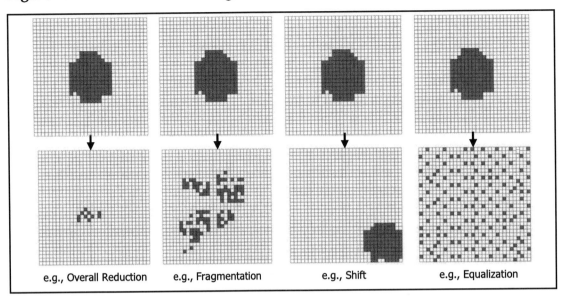

| e.g., Overall Reduction | e.g., Fragmentation | e.g., Shift | e.g., Equalization |

If the risk terrain methodology did not show any improvement to retrospective hotspot mapping, its added value to police operations would be negligible. Retrospective mapping is defined by using the locations of past events to forecast locations of future similar events. In police work, this univariate analysis assumes a static environment— that the locations of crimes do not change over time and it is operationalized as the production of density maps for visual analysis. A retrospective map of shootings, therefore, is a density map calculated from the locations of shooting incidents from Period 1 that would then be used to forecast the locations where shootings will occur during Period 2.

Risk terrain maps and retrospective maps must be produced and classified with the same parameters and technical procedures in order for direct comparisons to be made. For a case in point, and as exemplified in Figure 2, shooting incident locations were geocoded and then turned into a density raster map with cells classified using standard deviational breaks. Then each classification group was re-coded with a "risk" value from 0 (lowest risk; density values below the mean) to 3 (highest risk; density values greater than +2SD) using the "Reclassify" tool. (This procedure is explained in detail in Chapter 5, Step 7). As the map on the right side of Figure 2 shows, this procedure was also used to produce the risk map layer of "known gang members' residences" and all other risk factors for the comparison risk terrain maps. Shooting incidents from Periods 1 and 2 produced Period 1 and Period 2 retrospective maps, respectively. Since retrospective maps are based solely on one variable (e.g. shootings) their cells' risk values only range from zero to three (in this example). Clusters of cells with values of three are what might commonly be referred to as hotspots. It is assumed that a Period 1 retrospective map would correctly forecast the locations of some Period 2 shootings, and that a Period 2 retrospective map would correctly forecast the locations of some Period 3 shootings. While the predictive validity of retrospective maps is expected to be significant, as the existing literature suggests, it is hypothesized that risk terrain maps would have higher percentages of correct predictions.

Figure 2: Example of Risk Value Determination from Standard Deviation Classification Schema

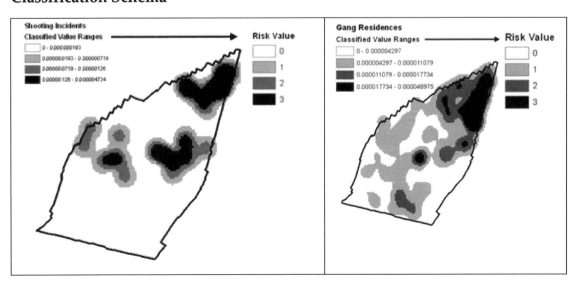

4,046 100ftX100ft cells comprised every map in this example. To ensure that the same number of highest risk cells was tested for each map (i.e. for comparison purposes) the top 10 percent (405), top 20 percent (810), top 30 percent (1,214) and top 40 percent (1,618) of cells were selected and designated as "High Risk" among four dichotomous variables, respectively. To do this in SPSS, rows in the attribute table of each map were sorted first by each cell's "Risk Value", and then by a random number, in descending order. To designate the top 10 percent of cells as high risk, for example, the first 405 sorted rows were selected and recoded into a new variable to identify these cells as "High Risk" and all other cells as "Not High Risk." This process was repeated for each (percentage) cut point and for all four maps (i.e. two risk terrains and two retrospective) so that each had the same number of cells designated as high risk. Finally, for each map, the count of shootings per cell was recoded into a dichotomous variable that noted the presence or absence of "any shootings".

The associations between high risk cells and shootings were tested for significance using 2x2 cross tabulations and Fisher's Exact Tests. Results for each cut point are presented in Table 1. As much as twenty-one percent more shootings occurred in high-risk cells forecasted by the risk terrain map compared to the retrospective map. The top 10 percent of high-risk cells in the Period 1 risk terrain map correctly forecasted 42% of future shootings, compared to 21% that were identified by the Period 1 retrospective map. This is a 100 percent increase in correct predictions—and possibly a conservative estimate of the risk terrain's potential because only three data layers were used to create risk terrains. As depicted in Figure 3, results suggest that risk terrains provide a statistically significant forecast of future shootings across all cut points, and are more effective than traditional hotspot mapping practices.

TABLE 1: Predictive Validity for Risk Terrain & Retrospective Maps			
	High-risk cell designation method (N=4046)	**% of cells with shootings during the following 6 months that were designated as high-risk (Period 1 n=24; Period 2 n=25)**	
		Risk Terrain Map	**Retrospective Map**
Period 1	Top 10%	42**	21
	Top 20%	54**	42*
	Top 30%	71**	63**
	Top 40%	75**	67*
Period 2	Top 10%	40**	28**
	Top 20%	56**	40*
	Top 30%	68**	52*
	Top 40%	80**	72**
*p<0.05 **p<0.01			

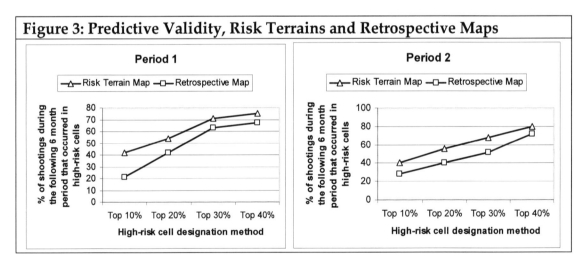

Figure 3: Predictive Validity, Risk Terrains and Retrospective Maps

Testing the Cohesiveness of Risk Terrain High-risk Cells

In examining the utility of risk terrain maps we can test for the cohesiveness of "risk clusters" they generate. This is important because risk terrain models will be of most operational utility to the police if they can create clearly defined clusters of high-risk cells that can be easily patrolled, as opposed to only a large number of dispersed isolate cells[53]. One way of measuring this is to conduct a Cluster and Outlier Analysis (Local Moran's I). For the purposes of operational policing, Local Moran's I is preferred to other hotspot analysis methods such as the Getis-Ord Gi* statistic (i.e. the "Hot Spot Analysis" tool in ArcGIS) because it can identify clusters of places with values similar in magnitude as well as features that are spatial outliers. For example, whereas the resultant Z score from the Getis-Ord Gi* statistic can only tell where features with either high or low values cluster spatially surrounded by other similarly-valued features, Local Moran's I can distinguish between statistically significant clusters of high values surrounded high values (HH), low values surrounded by low values (LL), high values surrounded by low values (HL), and low values surrounded by high values (LH).

This kind of information can be especially useful to police strategists within the context of risk terrain modeling because it allows for categorizing (and ultimately prioritizing) the most risky, most vulnerable, or least risky places. In police practice, this issue might be stated as: "We can continue with standard practices in places with zero (i.e. normal) risk, but where should interventions and police resources be directed to first and in the most efficacious way?" The answer is to focus on places with risk values greater than zero and on statistically significant clusters of HH, HL, and LH places since none of these places are (statistically) completely isolated from high-risk places and their criminogenic influences. Time and other resources permitting, further attention may be given to LL places.

> *Results suggest that risk terrain maps provide a statistically significant forecast of future shooting locations across all cut points, and are more effective than traditional hotspot mapping practices.*

Figure 4 shows results of a Local Moran's I test performed on a risk terrain map for shootings in Irvington, NJ. It is apparent from this map that risk can, in fact, cluster and that the nature of these clusters can better inform plans for police response. For example, officers might seek to leverage the social and human capital and other strengths of low-risk places that are nearby high-risk places in their efforts to mitigate one or more of the risk factors in both "risk cluster" spots. Or, because lower-risk clusters still have some criminogenic risk factors in them, police can monitor these places as they target nearby high-risk clusters to preempt any displacement or dispersion of risk factors (or new crime incidents) that could occur.

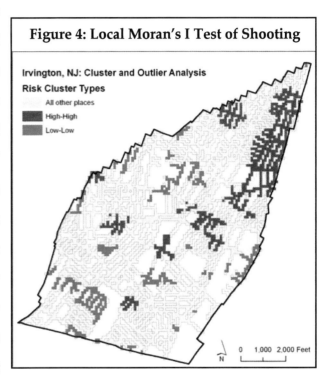

Figure 4: Local Moran's I Test of Shooting

Irvington, NJ: Cluster and Outlier Analysis
Risk Cluster Types
All other places
High-High
Low-Low

The map in Figure 4 only shows cells that intersected with streets because shooting incidents are recorded by street addresses in Irvington, NJ. That is, the exact locations of shooting incidents are unknown beyond the street name and number that was assigned to each incident. For example, if a shooting occurred in a back yard that was several hundred meters from the street in front of the house, the location of the shooting would nonetheless be recorded as the dwelling's street address. This is common practice for many police departments. For the purpose of modeling and testing risk terrains with real data, it was supposed that shootings could only occur on streets, and so the risk terrain map was constructed accordingly. This is also a practical model for operational policing since officers patrol along street segments—whether they drive, bike, or walk. Upon visual analysis of the map, police commanders might direct patrols to clusters of streets with high risk for shootings as a traditional form of deterrence.

In sum, risk terrain maps improve upon retrospective hotspot maps and produce evidence-based information that can be operationalized by police administrators easily and efficiently, such as for directing police patrols to coalesced high risk areas.

Using Both RTM and Hotspot Mapping for Police Operations

Hotspot density mapping of past events is a proven technology that does aid police operations and, while it is useful for tactical purposes in identifying areas for immediate police intervention, it is less useful for strategic planning or developing prevention-based operations. If a police department wants to target areas with existing high crime, then using simple retrospective density maps of these crimes will show the general areas where crime has been most concentrated and where it is suitable for common suppression methods (e.g. increase police patrols, ordinance enforcement, curfews, zero-tolerance enforcement of misdemeanors, knock & talks). But RTM grounds police operations in ecological theories of crime (already discussed in Chapter 1) and the mathematical theory of sparsity[54]. Ecological theories of crime support the conceptual framework of RTM and sparsity justifies the modeling of criminogenic places rather than always requiring absolute knowledge about every incident that already happened.

Consider the example of testing for syphilis during WWII[55]. Military recruiters had to very quickly test every new recruit, but they knew that individually testing everyone would be time consuming and costly. Instead, they drew blood from each recruit and mixed the samples among groups of 10 recruits and tested that one sample of mixed blood. Most of the time these tests were negative because syphilis was sparse among the general population; But, if a positive sample was found, they knew it belonged to at least one of the 10 recruits in the mixed-blood group. This procedure was grounded in the theory of sparsity because syphilis was relatively sparse in the population so using the groups-of-10 model to "compress" the samples for faster testing worked well. In fact, it worked just as well as testing every recruit separately would have, but without the added costs.

Crime, especially violent crime, is also relatively sparse in the population and throughout geographies. Not everyone is a criminal and violent crime does not happen everywhere. Even in cities where crime occurs more frequently than other cities, it tends to occur most often at certain places within the city and not at other places. For this reason, hotspot density mapping tends to be the operational default for directing police. Consider robbery, for example, which (though generally sparse) occurs often around major transit hubs. Criminological theory suggests that these places with a lot of suitable victims/targets are more likely to have robberies, and past crime statistics show that. Police can increase patrols and other interventions at transit stations in an effort to curb robberies. But, robberies also happen elsewhere in the city. How should police allocate the remaining limited resources to other parts of the city? If they direct resources to areas with many past robberies, they run the risk that these areas might not have similar amounts of future crimes, or that these crimes will be displaced to other areas that are just as conducive to crime, but less risky for criminals since they are (now) policed less. The challenge that police agencies face is to allocate resources to areas with high crimes in order to suppress them, and also to areas that pose the highest risk for crimes to occur in the future. Risk terrain modeling especially permits the latter. CompStat programs probably attempt to address both of these challenges but at worst fail completely or, at best, do not maximize the ability of police to succeed because they only focus on where crimes are or have been occurring, not where they could occur (even if they currently do not or historically have not occurred).

This encourages us to think more about using "risk clusters" instead of crime hotspots to allocate police resources, and we know (i.e. see the previous section) that RTM can generate this type of information. The risk clustering approach can direct police to anticipate crime problems early and address the correlates of crime outcomes. This is not a ridiculous supposition. Aspects of community-oriented policing, problem-oriented policing, and even CompStat programs, have tried to get police to think proactively and take preemptive action. Unfortunately, these principles for policing, while valuable and well intentioned, have not been supported enough by analytical techniques such as RTM and tangible information to direct police activities. If risk clusters do emerge, then RTM could ground risk-based policing much more into the spatial contexts in which police operate rather than focusing police on behavior that they are trying to control.

If retrospective hotspot mapping is combined with risk terrain modeling, crime analysts could identify places where crime is and is most likely to occur so that police commanders can immediately direct resources most efficiently and effectively. In addition, police can be more prepared for any displacement or disbursement to other high-risk (i.e. criminogenic) areas that might result from their targeted interventions. The success of police interventions at crime hotspots might even be evaluated by measuring increases or decreases of the targeted crime in places that police did not target, but where risk terrain models suggest would be the most conducive to future crime given the current high-risk clusters. For example, if crime decreases in the targeted areas and remains the same or decreases in other high-risk areas, the intervention might be considered a success. "Success" needs to be defined ahead of time so that an appropriate method of evaluation can be devised; though at the very least, RTM provides additional options for defining and measuring success. At its best, RTM accurately forecasts new crimes at specific places that are meaningful to police and manageable for targeted interventions. Police could assign resources accordingly to address one or more of the risk factors in the "risk cluster" spots while they focus suppression tactics at the (past) crime hotspots. With regard to the former, for example, they might institute community policing strategies that engage other municipal agencies and address problems of social disorganization, including the strict enforcement of ordinances related to vacant properties; public works departments might be instructed to limit roadway access to troubled areas, such as drug markets; and, parole officers might be consulted to better evaluate reentry plans of incarcerated offenders who will return to high-risk areas.

The risk clustering approach can direct police to anticipate crime problems early and address the correlates of crime outcomes.

Risk can in fact cluster, and the nature of these clusters can better inform plans for police response.

Steps and Techniques of Risk Terrain Modeling

CHAPTER THREE
A BASIC STEPWISE EXAMPLE OF RISK TERRAIN MODELING

STEP 1: Select an outcome event of particular interest.

Gun shooting incidents.

STEP 2: Decide upon a study area for which risk terrain maps will be created.

The Township of Irvington, NJ.

STEP 3: Choose a time period to create risk terrain maps for.

Six month time period: January 1 to June 30. It is expected that this time period will adequately assess the place-based risk of shootings during the next 6-month time period (July 1 to December 31).

STEP 4: Obtain base maps of your study area.

Two base maps were obtained from Census 2000 TIGER/Line Shapefiles: 1) Polygon shapefile of the Township and 2) Street centerline shapefile for the Township.

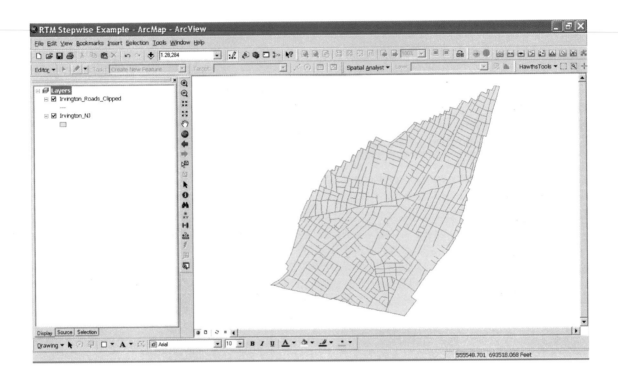

STEP 5: Identify aggravating and mitigating risk factors that are related to the outcome event.

Three aggravating factors were identified based on a review of empirical literature: dwellings of known gang members[56], locations of retail business infrastructure[57], and locations of drug arrests[58]. Dwellings of known gang members refers to addresses where police have information about one or more gang members residing; retail business infrastructure refers specifically to bars, strip clubs, bus stops, check cashing outlets, pawn shops, fast food restaurants, and liquor stores; drug arrests refers to arrests by police for drug sales or possession. (While drug arrests might be considered in some cases to be a proxy for police presence and an intervention strategy based on incapacitation and deterrence, here it is assumed that drug arrests at locations creates a void for new dealers to fill, which results in violent conflict at these places for control of territory).

STEP 6: Select particular risk factors to include in the risk terrain model.

All three risk factors identified in Step 5 will be included. Raw data in tabular form (i.e. Excel spreadsheets) was provided by the Township police and the many datasets they maintain, validate and update regularly to support internal crime analysis and police investigations.

STEP 7: *Operationalize risk factors to risk map layers.*

First, the tabular data was geocoded to street centerlines of Irvington to create point features representing the locations of gang members' residences, retail business outlets, and drug arrests, respectively as three separate map layers. (Note that the point features of "gang members' residences" is not shown in the screen capture below in order to protect the identification of these people and residences).

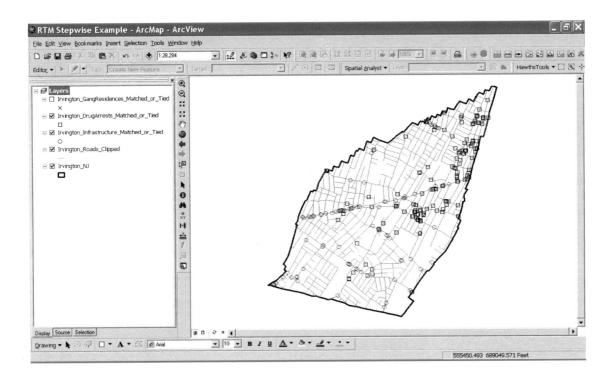

The spatial influence of the "gang members' residences" risk factor was operationalized as: "Areas with greater concentrations of gang members residing will increase the risk of those places having shootings." So, a density map was created from the points of gang members' residences.

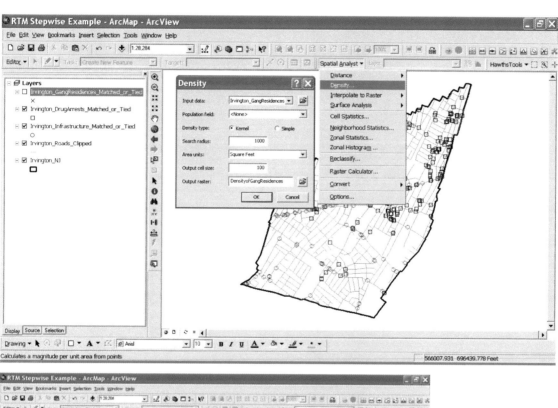

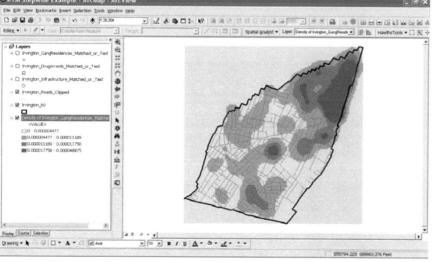

The spatial influence of the "infrastructure" risk factor was operationalized as: "High concentrations of bars, strip clubs, bus stops, check cashing outlets, pawn shops, fast food restaurants, and liquor stores will increase the risk of those dense places having shootings." So, a density map was created from the points of infrastructure.

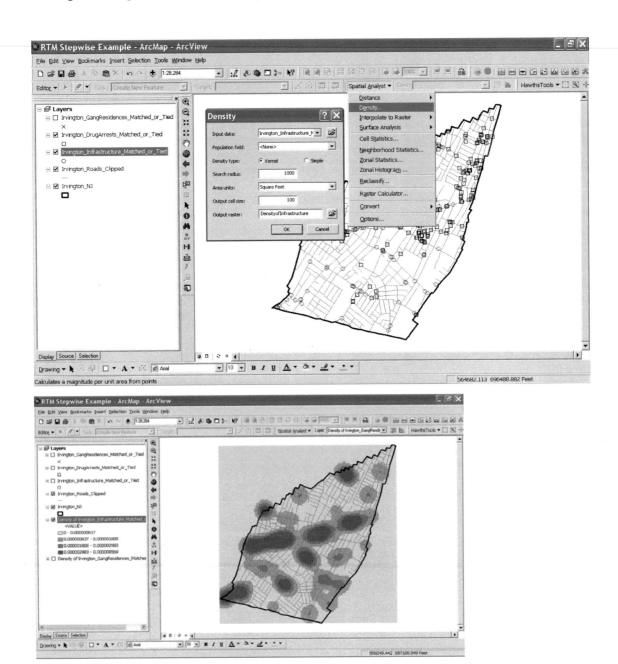

The spatial influence of the "drug arrest" risk factor was operationalized as: "Areas with high concentrations of drug arrests will be at a greater risk for shootings because these arrests create new 'open turf' that other drug dealers fight over to control." So, a density map was created from the points of drug arrests.

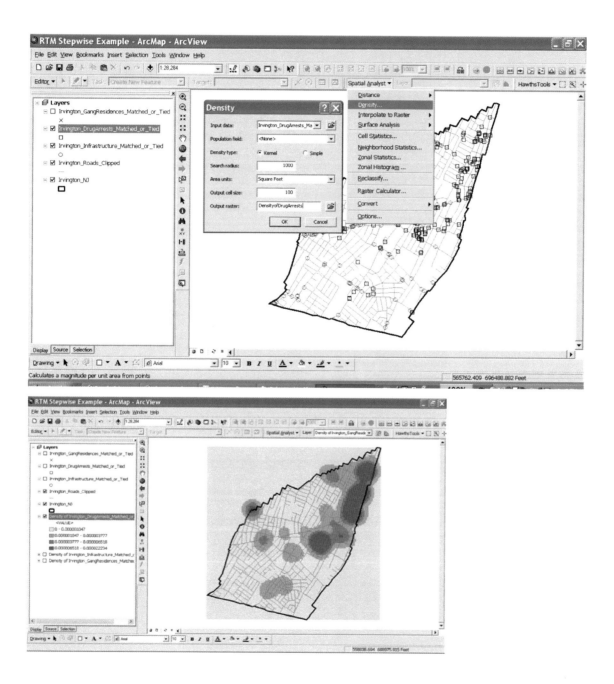

Kernel density values were calculated for each of the above risk map layers so that points lying near the center of a cell's search area would be weighted more heavily than those lying near the edge, in effect smoothing the distribution of values. The specific parameters for each of the three density calculations were a bandwidth of 1,000 feet and a cell size of 100 feet. A 1,000 foot bandwidth was selected because it seemed a reasonable sphere of influence for shooters—the average blockface is approximately 350 feet[59]. 100x100 foot cells were the smallest area that our computers could process reasonably fast and, for the purposes of this risk terrain model, if a risk terrain map could assess the risk of shootings at small (but reasonable) geographic units (e.g. 2 inches would be unreasonable since a person cannot even fit in that space), it would provide the most utility for operational policing compared to larger, less specific, units of analysis.

Cells within each density map layer were classified into four groups according to standard deviational breaks. The reason standard deviation was used as a classification scheme in this particular example is because it is not affected by positively skewed distributions or outliers, and it is statistically meaningful (i.e. greater than +2 SD is the Top 5%). Other schema, such as natural breaks, are less reliable for comparison purposes between map layers because they are very dependent upon the specific type of data and classification groups are not consistent across different map layers. Standard Deviation is much more robust and can be compared across maps. For all three map layers shown in the screen captures above, light blue colored cells had values below the mean cell value; cells colored light-medium blue had values between the mean and +1 standard deviation (SD); cells colored medium-dark blue had values between +1 SD and +2 SD; cells colored dark blue had values greater than +2 SD. In other words, the dark blue colored cells had values in the top five percent of the distribution and were considered the "highest risk" places.

The spatial influence of the "infrastructure" risk factor was also operationalized as: "The distance of one block, or about 350ft, from a facility poses the greatest risk of shootings because victims are often targeted when arriving at or leaving the establishment." So, a straight line distance map up to 350 feet from the points of infrastructure was created.

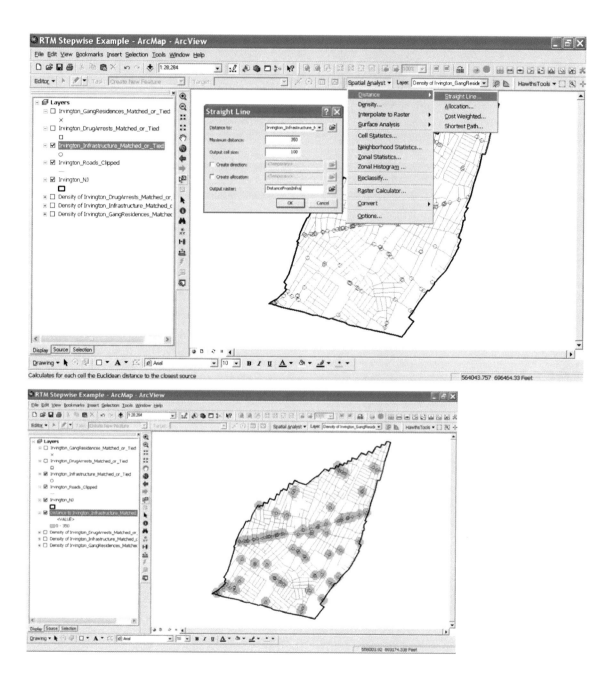

We are only interested in knowing where places are the most at risk for shootings, so we used a binary-valued schema to designate the "highest risk" places across all four risk map layers. The highest risk places of each risk map layer, respectively, will be given a value of "1"; all other places will be given a value of "0". All risk factors are operationalized as aggravating factors, so these values will remain positive. (Mitigating factors would be converted to negative numbers to represent their influence as reducing risk at places).

For the risk factors that were operationalized as density maps and classified according to standard deviational breaks, the "highest risk" places were deemed the cells with density values greater +2SD—or the top 5%. The "Reclassify" tool in the Spatial Analyst Extension was used to designate places with density values greater than +2SD as highest risk ("1") and all other places as not highest risk ("0"). This was done for each of the risk map layers (see screen captures on the following pages).

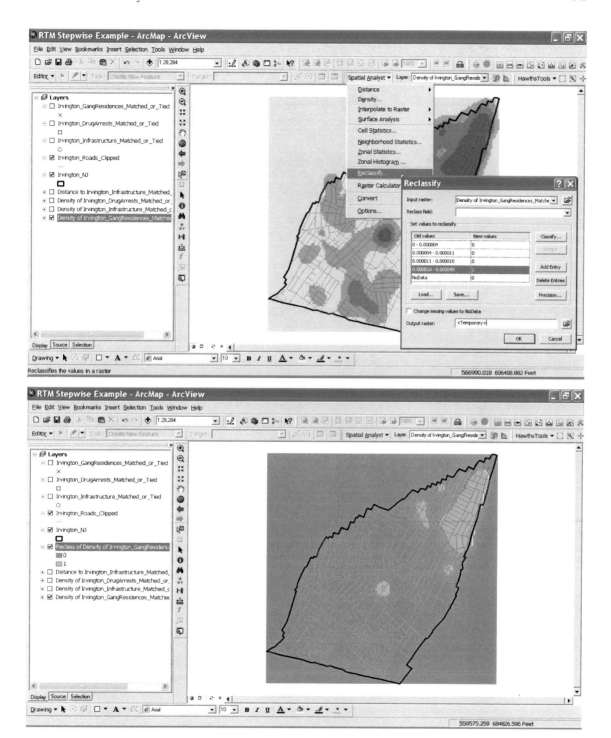

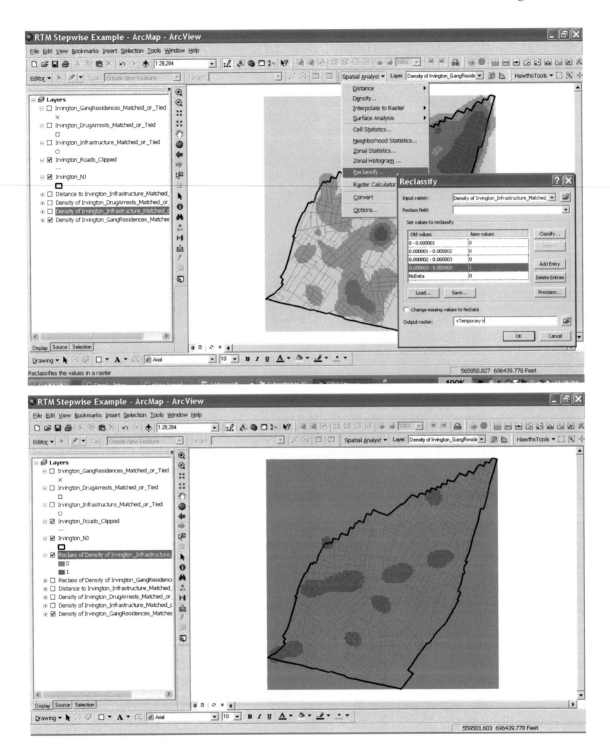

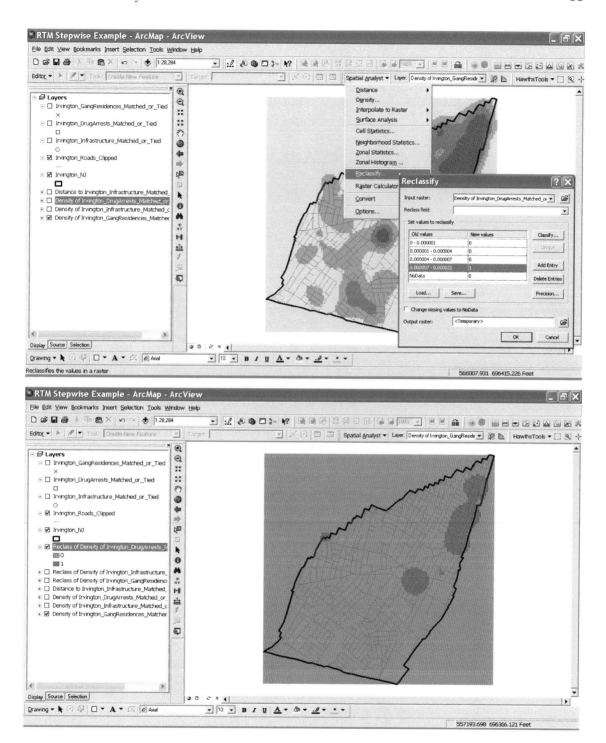

For the risk factor that was operationalized as distance from (infrastructure) points, the "highest risk" places were deemed the cells within 350ft from an infrastructure point.

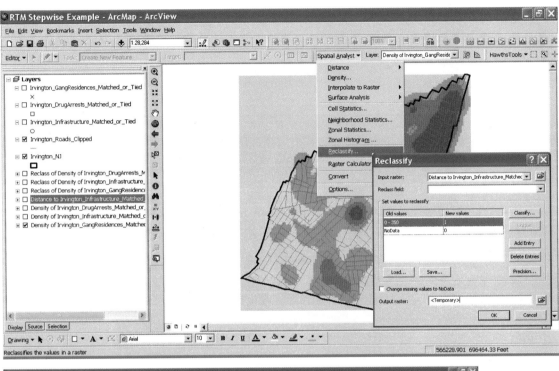

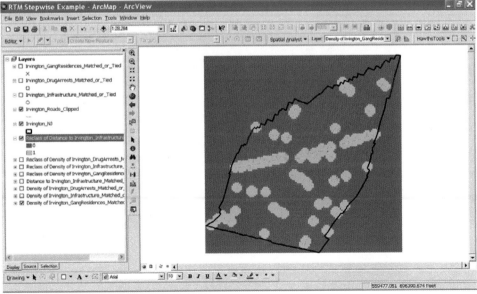

We now have four (final) risk map layers, operationalized from three risk factors. Every cell within each risk map layer was designated with a value of 1 or 0 according to whether the influence of the risk factor on that place makes it high risk or not high risk, respectively. Since the cells of different map layers are the same size and were classified in a standard/consistent way (i.e. 1 or 0), the risk map layers can be summed together to form a composite risk terrain map.

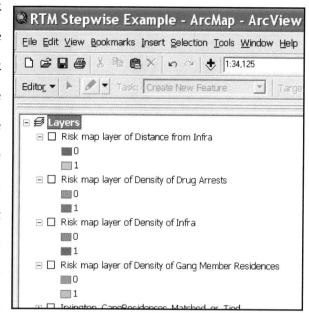

STEP 8: *Inter Risk Map Layer Weighting.*

All risk map layers will carry equal weights to produce an un-weighted risk terrain model. It is assumed, for example, that being in a place with a high concentration of drug arrests poses the same risk of having a shooting as being in a place with a high concentration of gang member residences.

STEP 9: Combine Risk Map Layers to Form a Composite Map.

(See www.rutgerscps.org/rtm/rastercalc.html for detailed steps to use Raster Calculator)

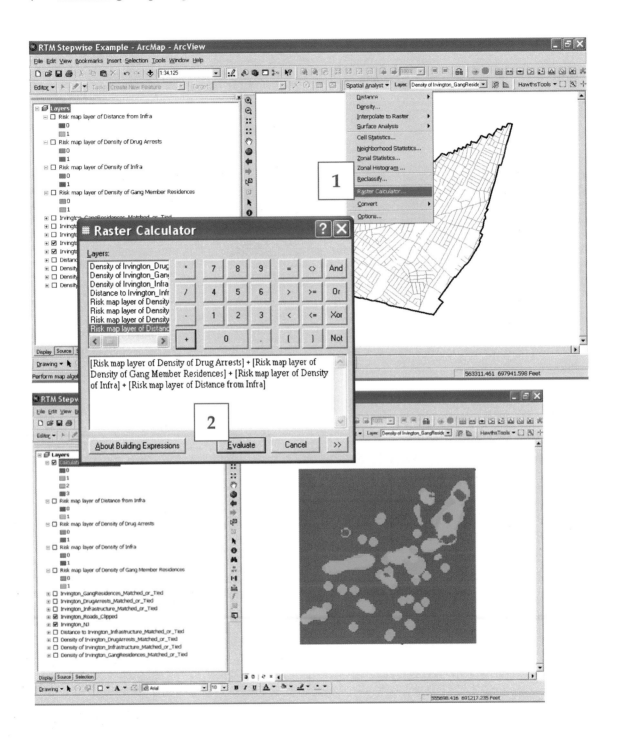

STEP 10: Finalize the Risk Terrain Map to Communicate Meaningful Information.

First, we want to clip our risk terrain map to the boundary of Irvington, NJ (see also www.rutgerscps.org/rtm/clipraster.html for detailed instructions).

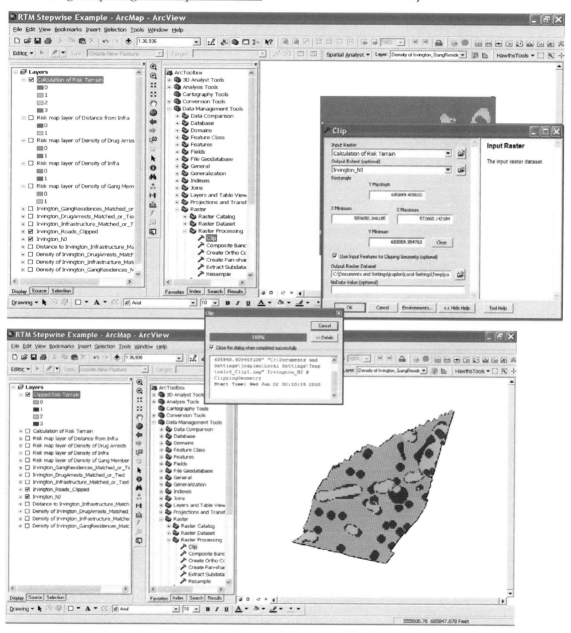

Now, we adjust the symbology to make a "Stretched" color ramp in shades of gray. Then we will produce a final map (with all necessary cartographic elements) in the Layout View of ArcMap (see www.rutgerscps.org/rtm/maplayout.html for detailed instructions and tips).

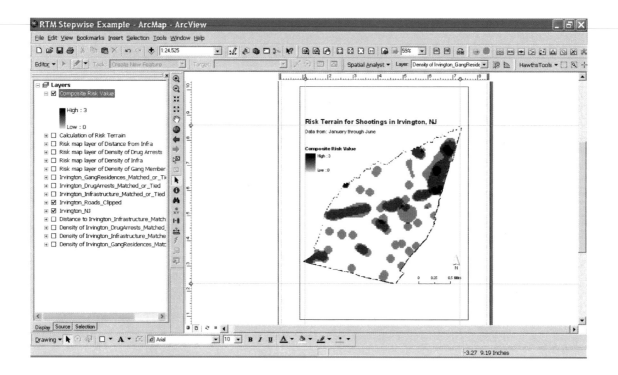

If we convert the risk terrain map from raster to vector (see screen capture below), we can: count the number of shootings that actually occur in the high-risk areas during the subsequent time period; calculate the square area of the highest risk areas (i.e., places with a composite risk value of 3); or use the "Select by Location" function in ArcMap to select all street segments within these areas to inform police commanders about where patrols might be increased (See examples below).

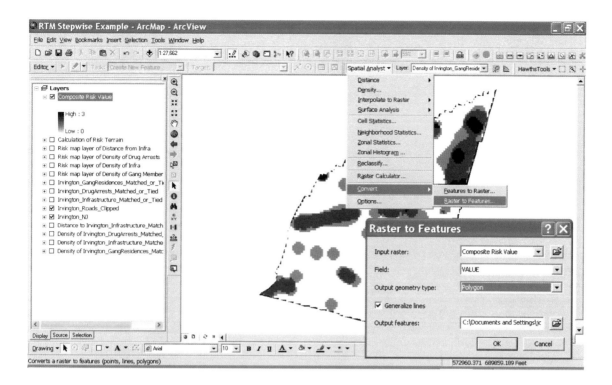

As an example, one piece of intelligence for strategic decision-making and police operations that can be derived from this risk terrain map might be: "Fifty block faces, totaling 4.2 miles, intersect with the high-risk areas for shootings. These include the 300 blocks of 16th Ave., the 100 blocks of 19th Ave., etc…. Interventions targeting one or more of the risk factors in the risk terrain model could be prioritized in these places and/or police car patrols might be increased on these streets as a traditional form of deterrence." (See screen capture below; Risk terrain maps depicting this information could be distributed to commanders and/or officers on patrol for further visual clarification).

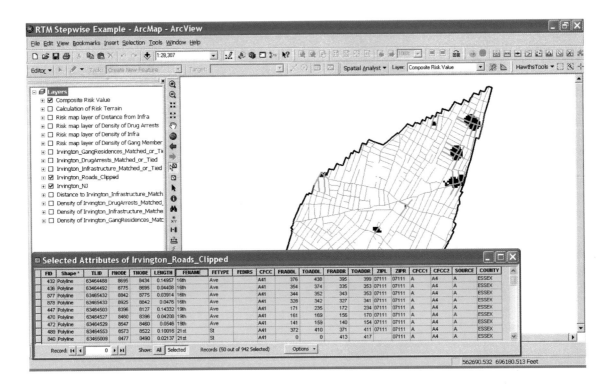

With a vector risk terrain map (converted from raster using the "Convert Raster Cells to Vector Polygon Grid" tool in the RTM Toolbox so that it preserves the integrity and value of each cell), we can also identify significant clusters of high-risk and low-risk places using the "Hotspot Analysis" tool in ArcMap. This could be used by police commanders for allocating resources and planning operations. In fact, the high-risk clusters shown in the screen capture below represent only 15.6% of the entire area of the Township of Irvington (2.8 square miles total); but about 50% (15 out of 31) of the shootings during the subsequent time period (July 1 to December 31) happened in these high-risk cluster areas. Prioritizing interventions to these high risk clusters could address nearly half of the shootings in the Township with only a fraction of police resources needed to patrol these places. As shown below, we started with a vector risk terrain comprised of 8,242 cells (100'x100' each) with composite risk values that ranged from 0 to 3 (highest risk).

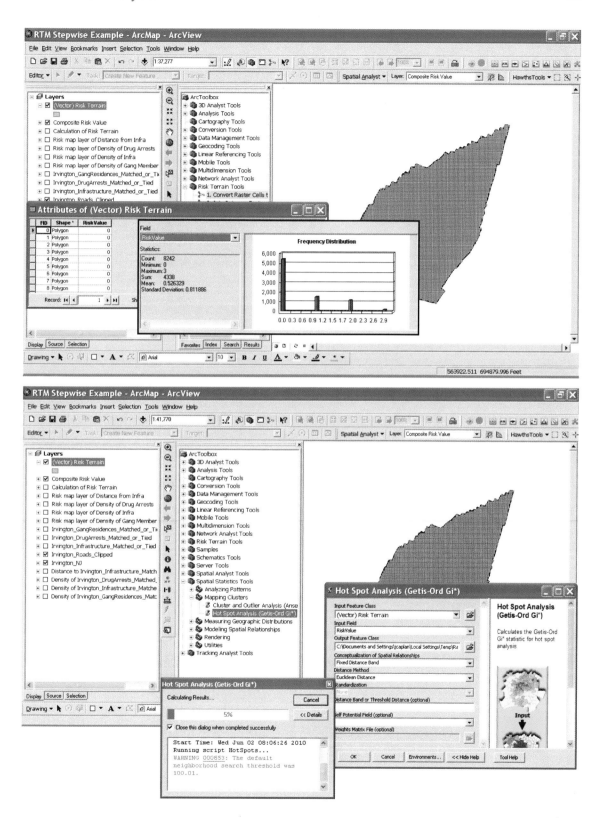

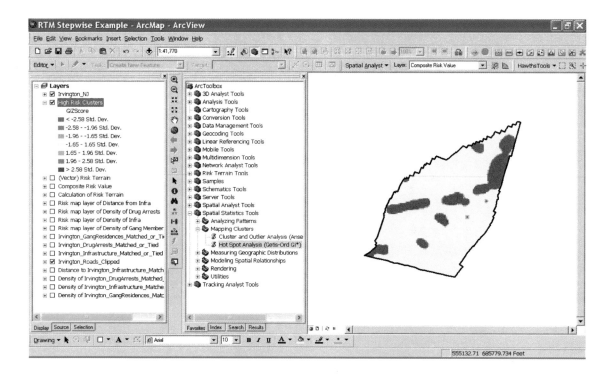

For a comparison of what might otherwise be used to direct police operations, the screen capture below shows a density map of shooting incidents from January 1 to June 30. Layered on top of the density map are the high-risk clusters (calculated with the "Hotspot Analysis" Tool using risk values of each place from the risk terrain map). Traditionally, police resources and interventions might be directed to hotspots of past shooting incidents, but as you can clearly see, our basic—un-weighted and binary-valued—risk terrain model shows much more specific and focused "priority areas", and it identifies some high-risk areas that might have otherwise gone unnoticed (in fact, shootings did subsequently gravitate towards them and occurred within one of them).

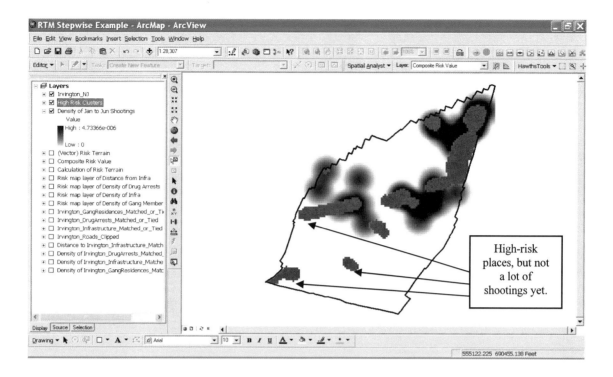

Remember, risk terrain modeling is only a tool for spatial risk assessment; it is not the solution to crime problems. You, the crime analyst, give value and meaning to RTM, so be innovative in your thinking about risk factors and how risk terrain maps can be applied to tactical and strategic police operations.

Risk terrain maps show much more specific and focused priority areas and identify high-risk places that might have otherwise gone unnoticed.

CHAPTER FOUR
GETTING STARTED WITH RTM

Introduction

Risk Terrain Modeling (RTM) is not difficult to do. An intermediate or advanced user of ArcGIS (or other software) might find the process easier than a novice, but this manual is intended to guide ArcGIS users with basic mapping skills and basic knowledge of vector and raster data through the technical and conceptual steps of RTM with minimal difficulty. For more detailed information or help with the technical aspects of ArcGIS, refer to the book "GIS for Public Safety: An Annotated Guide to ArcGIS Tools & Procedures," available for free PDF download at www.rutgerscps.org/gisbook. In this part of the manual, RTM is explained for the purpose of criminogenic risk assessment and forecasting; though, the RTM approach can also be used for purposes other than forecasting, such as for resource allocation or to evaluate the effects of past activities or interventions.

What You Need to Begin

- ArcGIS (or similar GIS software; you can get a free trial version at www.esri.com)
- Spatial Analyst Extension (or other raster processing tools)
- RTM Toolbox for ArcToolbox (free download at www.riskterrainmodeling.com)
- Spatial Data

Software: ArcGIS is a scalable system of GIS software produced by Environmental Systems Research Institute (Esri). This system contains three different products: ArcView, ArcEditor, and ArcInfo. Risk terrain modeling can be done with any of these products, but it does require the Spatial Analyst Extension. Note that ArcGIS is designed to run on a Microsoft Windows operating system. But with tools such as Parallels (www.parallels.com) or Boot Camp (part of MAC OS X Snow Leopard; www.apple.com), Intel-based Macintosh computer users can run ArcGIS products. (Just use an external mouse or learn how to "right-click" on a MAC).

If you do not already own ArcGIS Desktop, you may download a free trial copy at www.esri.com. The download includes a full version of the software at the ArcEditor license level, along with the Spatial Analyst Extension. If you are a student with a valid ID card, you might also consider purchasing the software at the discounted educational rate (as much as 80% off the regular price; contact the Educational and Government Discount representatives of Esri at 1-800-447-9778).

Spatial Analyst Extension: The Spatial Analyst Extension is specifically intended for the processing of grids (raster data) in ArcGIS. You will need the Spatial Analyst Extension and requisite toolbar to make risk terrain maps and work with raster data. Accessing the extension requires up to 3 steps (for more detailed steps with screen captures, see www.rutgerscps.org/rtm/SAE.html):

1. Install and Register the Spatial Analyst Extension

Whether you have a trial version or a full license of ArcGIS, you will need to install and register the Spatial Analyst Extension before creating density raster maps. To do this, go to Start > Programs > ArcGIS > Desktop Administrator. Select the "Register...Extensions" folder and then click the "Register Now" button. When the Registration Wizard appears, select the radio button next to "I have already registered the software and need to register additional ArcGIS extensions". Continue through the following registration screens, entering your user information as requested.

For trial version users (screens and options may differ slightly for fully licensed users): When you get to the "Evaluate ArcGIS Extensions" screen, click the radio button next to "I would like to evaluate one or more of the following extensions for a limited period of time." Then select the Spatial Analyst Extension by checking the box. Click the "Next" Button to continue with the registration. If you registered using the internet (recommended) you should receive a confirmation in the "Automatic Registration" screen as to what programs and extensions have been "Successfully registered and authorized". Click the "Finish" button and then exit out of ArcGIS Desktop Administrator.

2. Activate the Spatial Analyst Extension

Once extensions are installed and registered, you need to activate them. Open ArcMap and click Tools > Extensions. Check "Spatial Analyst" and then click the "Close" button.

3. Display the Spatial Analyst Toolbar

The Spatial Analyst Toolbar looks like this:
If the toolbar is not already visible, go to View > Toolbars, then select "Spatial Analyst".

Before you start working with raster data, you should define your study area by setting the analysis "extent" (From the "Spatial Analyst" toolbar, click "Spatial Analyst" button > Options > "Extent" tab; see also www.rutgerscps.org/rtm/extent.html). In the "Extent" tab of the "Options" dialog box, the default setting is likely to be "Intersection of Inputs." In the "Analysis extent" drop down menu, select an appropriate extent to meet your needs. If you want to use the same extent as another shapefile, such as your city's outline) add that shapefile layer to the Table of Contents in ArcMap first, then adjust the Analysis Extent: The drop down menu will provide an option for "Same as layer…". Click OK. Future density calculations will use this newly set extent. If you do not do this, you might notice that some of the areas on the raster maps that you created seem to be cut off. This occurs when the extent of the density calculation, for example, is limited to only the perimeter (i.e. extent) of the points that you are calculating the density of. Imagine this phenomenon as ArcGIS framing the output density raster map to only the smallest square box that includes all of the input points. Instead, you want the analysis extent to be the same as the entire study area (such as a city outline).

The process of risk terrain modeling is easier—both technically and conceptually—with raster data and the Spatial Analyst Extension and, therefore, raster mapping is the recommended method for risk terrain map production. But in the absence of the Spatial Analyst Extension, RTM could conceivably be done with vector data. If you understand the conceptual framework of RTM (e.g., simply put, the layering of risk factors to produce composite place-based risk values), then you should be able to improvise the steps using vector shapefiles. For example, you might start with a blank vector grid of equally-sized polygons (i.e. in place of a raster grid of cells) and then assign risk values as new attributes to each cell, respectively. Then, you could sum the attributes of each cell together to get a new "composite" risk value for each cell in the study area. Note that using vector data will likely result in slower computer processing times compared to raster data layers, especially for large study areas, and that some other limitations may apply.

RTM Toolbox and ArcToolbox: [From ArcMap or ArcCatalog, click the "ArcToolbox" button]. The ArcToolbox window is where you find, manage, and execute geoprocessing tools. Tools are (and must be) stored in Toolboxes, which are sorted alphabetically. The exact number of tools and toolboxes available depends on what extensions you have installed. The toolboxes you see in ArcToolbox are analogous to shortcuts in Windows Explorer or layers within ArcMap. If you remove a toolbox from ArcToolbox, you are simply removing it from the list and not actually deleting it on disk. BUT, if you delete a tool in a toolbox, the tool will be permanently deleted from the disk.

Opening Tools: [From the ArcToolbox window, double-click the tool].

Adding the RTM Toolbox to ArcToolbox: First download the Toolbox and save it to your computer's hard drive. [From the ArcToolbox window, right-click on the ArcToolbox > Add Toolbox > navigate to the folder with the Toolbox, select it > Click the "Open" button].

Spatial Data (Shapefiles, Vector and Raster Data): Data are essential to GIS and base maps are the foundation. Essentially, base maps are your reference layers for orienting and analyzing your primary data. Typically, they comprise a street centerline and a geographic backdrop such as a county or city boundary. Street centerlines of almost every city, state, or region can be downloaded free from the Internet (see Census

TIGER/Line® Data: http://arcdata.esri.com/data/tiger2000/tiger_download.cfm). City planning departments also often have GIS data (such as updated street files) that they may be willing to share. Remember, you want to obtain "shapefiles" if possible, which are the most compatible forms of data for use in a GIS. If shapefiles are not already available that is OK, you can create them. But, the data—whether it is your own or from another agency—must have a geographic reference such as street addresses or XY coordinates that can be used to link it to a map.

Shapefiles: Environmental Systems Research Institute (Esri; the maker of ArcGIS) created the shapefile format in order to represent vector GIS data. Other GIS programs will use shapefiles, but geographic files from other GIS programs must be converted to shapefiles before ArcGIS applications can read them. As with other formats of geographic data, shapefiles link information about the location and shape of the map features to their attributes.

Vector Data: Vector is a common format for GIS data used in the social sciences. It uses points, lines, and polygons to represent map features. Vector data is excellent for representing discrete objects such as parcels, streets, and administrative boundaries. The vector format is not as good for representing things that vary continuously over space, such as temperature, elevation, or risk.

Raster Data: Raster data use grids made up of regularly-sized cells to represent spatially continuous data. Each cell is assigned real world coordinates and one attribute value (such as risk value). The user defines the cell size, allowing for very fine or course raster surfaces. Even when the cell size is very small, you can see the individual square cells when you zoom in. Raster grid cells are like pixels on a TV or computer screen.

Whereas vector shapefiles are oriented toward the depiction and analysis of discrete objects in space (represented as points, lines, or polygons), raster grids are oriented more toward the qualities of space itself. In order to work with raster data in ArcGIS, you need the Spatial Analyst Extension. When raster layers have the same size cells, their values can be added, subtracted, multiplied, divided and queried using map algebra and the Raster Calculator in ArcGIS's Spatial Analyst Extension.

CHAPTER FIVE
STEPS OF RISK TERRAIN MODELING

A Really Brief Overview of the Steps of RTM

☐ Identify risk factors for a particular outcome event.

☐ Operationalize risk factors to risk map layers.

☐ Combine risk map layers to produce a composite risk terrain map.

Detailed Steps of Risk Terrain Modeling

Every effort should be made to maximize validity and reliability of your risk terrain model. The discussions that follow each step below are intended to provide some guidance as you consider these methodological issues, and to explain the conceptual and technical purpose of each step in relation to all subsequent steps in the risk terrain modeling process.

It is recommended that your first risk terrain map be done using binary-valued risk map layers (see Step 7) and an equal-weights risk terrain model (see Step 9). This is the easiest risk terrain map to produce and it is best for practicing the technical and conceptual aspects of risk terrain modeling. If this "basic" map proves useful and/or is found to have statistically significant predictive validity, then it may be considered a conservative estimate of your risk terrain model's potential. You can then revise your model, apply weights, or incorporate other more advanced techniques to improve your risk terrain maps as needed.

STEP 1: Select an outcome event of particular interest.

(e.g. shooting incidents, burglaries, auto thefts)

Risk terrain modeling is a form of spatial risk assessment that is specific to the outcome event of interest. If you are interested in assessing the risk of more than one event or type of crime, then you will get the most reliable results if you repeat the steps presented here to produce separate risk terrain models for every event (or, at least one risk terrain model for groups of events with similar underlying risk factors). This might sound impractical, but it is reasonable. For example, the causes of bicycle thefts most likely differ from the causes of shootings, so you would not generally combine bicycle theft and shooting events together to identify mutual risk factors. More generally, it would not be reasonable to use a risk terrain map of murders to forecast the locations of bicycle thefts because the risk factors for each differ.

STEP 2: Decide upon a study area for which risk terrain maps will be created.

(e.g. municipal boundary, police jurisdiction, statewide, global)

One advantage of risk terrain modeling is that it can be applied to any extent—small or large. Conceivably, if you want to assess the risk of finding a needle in a haystack, your study area could be the haystack; or, if you want to assess the risk of maritime piracy on the Earth's oceans, your extent could be the entire globe. The only real limit to the study area you select is your ability to obtain data for all of it.

When deciding upon a study area, you should consider at least three things. First, select an area for which the information provided by the risk terrain will be meaningful for operational management. For example, if you are a crime analyst for Springfield Police Department (SPD), then your study area might be the jurisdictional boundary of SPD. But, if SPD is part of a county-wide taskforce to suppress open-air drug markets, then the extent of your risk terrains for drug markets would be the entire county.

Second, make sure that your risk factors data and all base maps will cover the entire study area that you select, and that your outcome event data (i.e. shooting incidents) is collected/recorded in a manner that covers the entire area. For instance, the Newark Police Department (NPD) is responsible for policing most areas in the City of Newark, NJ. One exception is the Newark Liberty International Airport. Because the NPD does not record or collect data for crime incidents that fall under the jurisdiction of airport law enforcement authorities, a risk terrain for Newark PD should exclude areas under airport jurisdiction to yield a study area that is more accurately representative of the NPD's operational jurisdiction.

Finally, be careful not to select a study area that is too large for, or unrepresentative of, the outcome event since this can produce both visually and statistically deceptive results. For instance, if you are assessing the spatial risk of assault on college campuses in Newark, NJ, then your study area should not be the entire geopolitical boundary of the city of Newark. Rather, it should only include areas that are part of a college campus and exclude all other areas. Visually, failure to exclude non-college campus areas would encourage the eyes to focus on clusters of high-risk within the city (i.e. college campuses) instead of the intended micro-level assessment of high-risk places within college campuses. Statistically, failure to exclude non-college campus areas would include all of these places into the statistical test of predictive validity of your risk terrain model even though those places cannot (by definition) have a "college campus assault" occur within them. This could skew your results and would result in an underestimation of your model's validity.

STEP 3: *Choose a time period to create risk terrain maps for.*

(e.g. one week, six months, one year).

The time period should be meaningful for your data and considerate of how the information communicated by the risk terrain map will be used for decision-making (i.e. long-term, short-term). For example, if a task force will be implementing an intervention next year to prevent and suppress new and existing drug markets over the course of the entire year, then a risk terrain map produced with data from January 1 through December 31, 2010 (Period 1) might be used to make strategic decisions about where to allocate resources during all of 2011. Or, if a risk terrain model will be used on a weekly basis to (re)direct police patrols to high-risk areas in response to a recent spate of burglaries, then a risk terrain map produced with data from Week 1 might be used to assign patrols during Week 2, and so on.

You should be able to reasonably justify that the qualities of the study area during time period 1 are (or will be) relevant during the subsequent time period that you are trying to model. As an extreme example, it is probably not reasonable to use a risk terrain map that was produced with data from one week during the summer in 2010 to forecast risky locations during the entire 2011 calendar year because for many reasons a summer week is not representative of happenings throughout an entire year. This example raises the issue of seasonality. The time period that you choose may depend on seasons. For instance, certain types of events, such as bicycle thefts, are more likely to occur during warmer months of the year (i.e. in places where winters are cold). You might, then, make a risk terrain map with data from "Summer" 2010 to forecast high-risk locations for bicycle thefts during "Summer" 2011. Maritime terrorism is another example of how seasonality could affect time periods used for RTM because empirical research suggests that the frequency of maritime pirate attacks changes according to the weather conditions. There are fewer pirate attacks during monsoon season, for example. If you wanted to create a risk terrain map of global maritime piracy for an entire calendar year, you would actually have to create separate risk terrain maps using data from each of the seasons to produce each map, respectively. In effect, this would "control" for seasonality. The "Monsoon Season Risk Terrain Map" using risk factors from the 2010 monsoon season might be used to forecast risky locations of maritime pirate attacks during the 2011 monsoon season. But, this map would not yield as reliable or valid measures of risky places during a season with calmer waters.

Basically, the time period is important for interpreting risk terrain maps in a valid, meaningful, and actionable way.

STEP 4: Obtain base maps of your study area.

You will need, at a minimum, a polygon shapefile of your study area. This will be used to clip the risk terrain map to the exact limits of your study area. As Figure 5 exemplifies, raster mapping produces a rectangular grid of cells that can extend beyond your specific study area. The polygon shapefile of your study area can be used to clip the risk terrain map (using the "Clip" tool in ArcGIS; see www.rutgerscps.org/rtm/clipraster.html) to the exact boundary of your study area. This is important for aesthetics and to clearly communicate high- and low-risk areas in places that matter. If you intend to statistically test the predictive validity of your risk terrain map, then clipping "irrelevant" cells is also important because those cells have no real data in them, which could bias your results.

Figure 5: Example of how a shapefile can be used to clip a risk terrain map

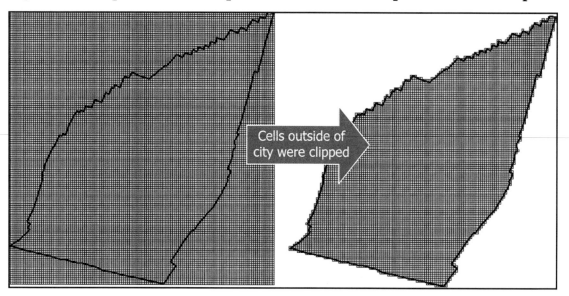

As discussed in Step 2, you might choose to obtain shapefiles of areas where data will be excluded from your risk terrain map, such as airports under a separate jurisdiction from the city police. A written notation or a map feature showing the airport area could improve the communicability and visual clarity of your final risk terrain maps because they can aid the map reader in understanding why some areas have zero risk, missing data, or no outcome events. Another useful base map could be street centerline shapefiles for geocoding addresses of risk factors (such as locations of schools, bars, or bus stops) to points on a map. Other base maps, such as parks, waterways, or forested areas—if not already used as risk factors in your risk terrain model—could be used as reference layers in the design of your final map to give readers better geographic context.

At least some base maps that you may need are readily available for free in GIS-compatible formats via public sources. Census 2000 TIGER/Line shapefiles that were created from the Topologically Integrated Geographic Encoding and Referencing

(TIGER; http://arcdata.esri.com/data/tiger2000/tiger_download.cfm) database of the United States Census Bureau is a source for most infrastructure and geography variables such as roads, highways, and land-use. This can be supplemented with decennial census data about households, income, education, homeownership, vacant properties and other variables downloaded from the US Census Bureau's American FactFinder (http://factfinder.census.gov).

To maximize the validity and reliability of your risk terrain model, use base maps that are the most representative of the time period that you are creating risk terrain maps for. If you are using risk terrain modeling to evaluate a completed intervention, then you might require older maps (e.g. new roads are added all the time). If you are producing risk terrain maps to identify future risky places, then you probably want to use the most current data and base maps (remember, census data can be as much as 10 years old!).

STEP 5: Identify aggravating and mitigating risk factors that are related to the outcome event.

The product of this step should be a comprehensive list of risk factors that are related to the outcome event in your study area. For example, if you are creating a risk terrain model for auto theft, your list might include: parking lots, street lighting, train stations, chop shops, registered addresses of Toyota Camry owners, etc. Fortunately, empirical research has already identified a variety of independent variables to be significantly correlated with a variety of crime outcomes. Risk terrain modeling enables the crime analyst to simultaneously apply all of these empirical findings to practice.

Your scholarly prowess, access to empirical literature, and innovativeness are key components of how comprehensively you can identify all factors that are related to the crime for which risk is being assessed. Some suggestions are: meta-analysis or other empirical methods, literature review, professional experience, and practitioner knowledge[60]. Ideally, you want to identify every single aggravating and mitigating factor to include in your risk terrain model. Though practically, this is neither feasible nor possible, and that's OK. At the very least, make a reasonable effort to identify as many factors that you believe to be related to the outcome event in your particular study area. Different crimes will likely have different risk factors; or, different risk factors might be identified for the same type of crime in completely different settings. For example, risk factors of shootings in large cities might differ from risk factors of shootings in small towns.

If you have access to a college or university library, search the catalog and electronic journal databases for books and articles related to your outcome event and that suggest risk factors relevant to your study area. You can also search Google Scholar (http://scholar.google.com), which indexes scholarly literature across many disciplines and sources (and it is free!). Another option is to look at reports and documents from reputable research centers such as the Urban Institute (http://www.urban.org), the Center for Problem Oriented Policing (www.popcenter.org), the Campbell Collaboration (www.campbellcollaboration.org), or the US DOJ Office of Community Oriented Policing Services (http://www.cops.usdoj.gov). Presentation abstracts and professional conference proceedings are another useful source of general information about your outcome event (e.g., see www.acjs.org or www.asc41.com). You might also join the International Association of Crime Analysts (IACA; www.iaca.net) electronic discussion list to confer with experienced practitioners. There are many sources of reliable information about risk factors related to your outcome event—too many to list all of them here. Consult those that are most accessible and useful to you.

STEP 6: Select particular risk factors to include in the risk terrain model.

Your ability to use every risk factor in the final risk terrain map might be possible. However, chances are that your ability to use every risk factor from the list that you compiled in Step 5 will be limited by the availability or quality of data. Sometimes, this is due to the nature of your jurisdiction. For example, research has suggested that the locations of burglaries are correlated with the incident locations of future shootings[61]. If your city has very few or zero recorded burglaries, then that risk factor might be irrelevant and excluded from your risk terrain model of shootings. Other times, you might be forced to exclude a risk factor from the model because of missing data. For example, research has also suggested that the locations of bars and other liquor establishments are correlated with the locations of shooting incidents. If you are unable to obtain a list of these liquor establishments—or if the list you have is incomplete or unreliable—you might have to produce a risk terrain map without this risk factor (or find a proxy measure). Risk terrain modeling is dependent upon the availability of valid data from reliable sources.

More risk factors do not always produce better models. Just because your literature review identified seven factors to be correlated with the outcome event, for example, including all seven factors in the risk terrain model might not yield a risk terrain map with the best predictive validity. The model may still be meaningful and could serve your operational needs, but improvements to the model might come from including only the "most correlated" factors and excluding all others. This phenomenon of "less-can-be-more" in RTM has been proved empirically by Kennedy, Caplan and Piza (see research brief at http://www.rutgerscps.org/Publications.htm#briefs) in their work with risk terrain modeling in Newark, NJ, but it also makes intuitive sense. For example, policing scholars have long been concerned with the generalizability of empirical research to different geopolitical jurisdictions and settings. Social, political, economic and cultural characteristics of New York City (NYC) are arguably different than New Orleans, for example, so the conclusions drawn from research in NYC about correlates of a particular type of crime might not be applicable to New Orleans or any other settings. As you identify risk factors to include in a risk terrain model, just remember that local variations in criminogenic risk can exist. You should strive to compile an exhaustive list of possible risk factors, but, for various reasons, you might not include all of those factors in your final risk terrain model. As Kennedy et al. realized about shootings in Newark, the best risk terrain model may result from using only three risk factors out of a list of seven. Two methods for deciding which factors to include and which ones, if any, to exclude, are discussed below.

Both options (discussed below) for selecting risk factors to include in a risk terrain model have their strengths and weaknesses. The ad-hoc method is based solely on the assumption that findings from various sources about what to include in your risk terrain model are valid and applicable to your study area. There is no further statistical verification or justification used. This method is advantageous because it allows for expedient risk terrain map production that is grounded in existing theory, empirical research, and/or professional experience. But, it lacks the statistical support that your model is in fact the best of many alternatives in your particular study area. The ad-hoc method is likely to be an appropriate option for risk terrain modeling by many crime analysts in many settings.

The <u>empirical method</u> requires an extra step of statistical analysis <u>and</u> a dataset of outcome event locations. This extra step empirically tests the place-based correlation of each risk factor (that you identified in Step 5) on the outcome event. This permits the use of only the most significantly correlated risk factors in your risk terrain model. The downside to the empirical method is the time required to complete it and the need for outcome events (which you might not have; though, you can use outcome event data from the same time period as the risk factor data. The outcome events do not have to be "future" events). The advantage of the empirical method is that it helps to maximize the reliability and validity of your risk terrain model by permitting the inclusion of only the most relevant risk factors.

Ad-hoc Method of Risk Factor Selection: Something isn't always better than nothing, but in the case of risk terrain modeling, it could be. If it makes sense to include all of the risk factors that you identified in Step 5, then do it. If your knowledge of the study area, personal experience, and/or data limitations reasonably justifies the inclusion of only some of the many risk factors that you identified, then use only those factors. Or, through an iterative process of trial-and-error, you might realize the best model after producing a risk terrain map, testing it for predictive validity (either statistically—see Chapter 6, or via pragmatic/experiential means), and then comparing it to subsequent risk terrain maps produced with different combinations of risk factors. These are all ad-hoc methods for creating risk terrain models.

The ad-hoc method should be supported (at a minimum) with a reasonable and articulable justification for why certain factors were included in your risk terrain model. Your goal should be to maximize the credibility, validity and reliability of the risk terrain maps that will ultimately be produced by the combination of risk factors that you select.

Empirical Method of Risk Factor Selection: Objectively choosing some risk factors out of many to include in your risk terrain model requires a series of statistical tests to assess the strength of place-based correlations between each risk factor and the outcome event. The statistically-faint-of-heart might elect to stick with the ad-hoc method of model building. However, empirical methods have the unique ability to maximize the validity of the model with a certain degree of statistical confidence.

We recommend using a series of Chi-squared tests to identify the variables most significantly correlated with the outcome event. So, for example, imagine a risk terrain model of shooting incidents in which you initially identified seven risk factors: First, operationalize all of them as separate "risk map layers" (see Step 7). For example, if being within 200ft from a liquor store is considered high-risk, then make a map layer with 200ft buffers around all liquor store points; if bus stops are high-risk, then make another map with points of all bus stops; and so on. Also make a separate map with points of all the incident locations of the outcome events—in this case, a point map of shootings. For all of these maps, use data from the time period that you selected in Step 3.

Next, create a blank vector grid of cells that covers the entire study area (from Step 2). (The "Create Vector Grid Tool" in Hawth's Analysis Tools for ArcGIS is a convenient way to do this: http://www.spatialecology.com/htools/createvectorgrid.php, or use your own method). Make sure that the cell sizes of this grid are the same size that will be used for your risk terrain maps (see the third paragraph of Step 7 regarding cell size selection).

The objective is to assign attributes to the vector grid cells that note whether a cell intersects with any of the features on the "risk map layers". This can be done with several functions in ArcGIS, but the most common are "Spatial Joins" or "Select by Location" (see www.rutgerscps.org/rtm/joinloc.html for detailed instructions). You can spatially join all shooting incidents to the vector grid to get a count of shootings per cell. Then add a new field in the attribute table [Options > Add Field] and note whether each cell has "any shootings" (i.e. 1 or more shootings) or "no shootings" (i.e. zero shootings). Another option would be to use the "Select by Location" function in ArcMap to "select all cells of the vector grid that 'intersect' with point features on the shooting map". Then add a new field in the attribute table of the vector grid and assign all "selected" cells a value of "1" (i.e. a shooting happened there), then "Switch Selection" to assign all other cells a value of "0" (i.e. no shooting happened there). [Tip: use the Field Calculator to quickly assign values: Right click the column heading > Field Calculator].

To continue from the example above, use the "Select by Location" function in ArcMap to "select all cells of the vector grid that 'intersect' with the 200ft buffer features of the liquor store risk map layer." Then assign attribute values to all selected and unselected cells, respectively, to note which cells have a "liquor store risk" and which cells do not. Repeat this process for all risk map layers and the outcome event. For this particular example, the end product would be a vector grid shapefile with an attribute table that has eight new variables, each noting the presence or absence of one of the seven risk factors and any shootings (i.e. the outcome event) in each cell.

Next, export the attribute table of the vector grid as a DBF file and import it into a software application that can create cross tabulation tables and perform Chi-squared (or Fisher's Exact) tests, such as SPSS or Microsoft Excel[62]. (To learn more about Chi-squared tests, see: http://faculty.chass.ncsu.edu/garson/PA765/chisq.htm or http://itl.nist.gov/div898/handbook/eda/section3/eda35f.htm). For this example, seven Chi-squared tests would be done on seven separate 2x2 tables. The unit of analysis is "cells" (i.e. places) within your study area. So the cross tabulations will tell you the percentage of cells that had the risk factor and shootings present. Upon review of these results, select only the risk factors that were significantly correlated with shootings (i.e.

p-value is 0.05 or less) and only the factors where the percentage of cells with both the outcome event and the risk factor was greater than the percentage of cells with a risk factor but no outcome event (as exemplified in Table 2).

Table 2		Any Shooting Incident (outcome event)	
		No	Yes
Liquor Store Risk (risk factor)	No	95.8%	71.8%
	Yes	4.2%	28.2%

STEP 7: Operationalize risk factors to risk map layers.

The objective here is to create separate raster maps of your study area, each representing the influence of a risk factor throughout the geography. You will need at least as many maps (herein referred to as 'risk map layers') as there are risk factors in your risk terrain model. You will have at least one risk map layer for each risk factor that represents the presence, absence, or intensity of the risk factor at places throughout your study area.

It is also possible that one risk factor might be operationalized into more than one risk map layer. For example, assume that a risk factor for robbery is "liquor stores". Liquor stores might influence the environment (relative to robbery) in a variety of ways, so a risk map layer of each way should be created. High-risk might be operationalized as being within 200ft of a liquor store, so a risk map layer of 200ft buffers around liquor stores would be created. Another level of high-risk places might also be operationalized as areas where there are many liquor stores together, so a risk map layer representing areas with high density of liquor stores would also be created. The theoretical and technical process of operationalizing risk factors to risk map layers is discussed in more detail below. Just be aware of the difference between a risk factor and the operationalization of that risk factor to the geography that is influenced by it. The influence can be justified by the results of existing empirical research, industry literature/reports, professional experiences, or some other credible sources. Simply put, operationalizations of risk factors to risk map layers should make sense.

By the end of this step, all risk map layers must be (converted to) raster, as discussed below. If you have not done so already, now is a good time to decide what the raster cell sizes should be. Technically, cell size determines how coarse or smooth the raster maps will appear; the smaller the cell size, the smoother the map will be. However, very small cells require considerably more processing time and computer storage space, especially if your study area is large. Conceptually, the cell size you select should make sense and be meaningful for operational purposes. For example, RTM was applied in Newark, NJ with a cell size of 140 feet because that is half the average block length in the city. It was believed that about one block was a reasonable area for crime events to happen within and was small enough for targeted interventions should risk in these areas be found to be high. As extreme examples, a cell size of 2 inches would be unreasonable since a person cannot even fit in that space and a cell size of 10 miles would not be meaningful for operational policing given the vast area within each cell. Exceptionally large cell sizes could also create problems regarding the phenomenon of "edge effects." Ultimately, the cell size is a subjective decision that should be based on how precise your risk assessment needs to be—the smaller the cell size the better the precision (as long as your risk factor data is also precise, e.g., point-level data). The general rule-of-thumb is to select a cell size that will enable actionable interpretations of risk terrain maps.

The process of operationalizing each risk factor to a risk map layer should be done so that it reasonably and meaningfully represents the influence of the risk factor on the outcome event at each place throughout the study area. If "night clubs" are a risk factor for shootings, then you might operationalize night clubs as "areas with higher concentrations of night clubs will be at higher risk for shooting incidents" and, thus, create a density raster map of night clubs in your study area. In this case, the resulting risk map layer would be a raster map (if you used the "Density" function in the Spatial Analyst Extension). Ultimately, all risk map layers must be in the form of raster data and the cell size must be exactly the same across every risk map layer. If the first step of your operationalization does not produce a raster map layer, then you must convert the vector risk map layers to raster (using the "Convert Features to Raster" function in the Spatial Analyst Extension in ArcMap).

Once all risk map layers are in raster form, symbolize each layer with a classification scheme that groups each cell in a meaningful way. For instance, if being within 500ft of an ATM is operationalized as high risk for robbery and all other places farther away are operationalized as being low risk, then your "ATM risk map layer" would be classified with two categories: 1) all cells within a distance of 500ft from the nearest ATM, and 2) all cells greater than 500ft from an ATM. Or, to continue from the example above: if being at a place with a "night club density value" that is greater than +2 Standard Deviations is considered the highest risk, being less than +2 SD but above the mean is considered medium risk, and being below the mean is considered low risk, then your "night club risk map layer" would be classified with three categories: 1) all cells with density values above +2 SD, 2) all cells with density values between the mean and +2 SD, and 3) all cells with density values below the mean.

The "ATM risk map layer" (mentioned above) is an example of a binary-valued risk map layer. This means that every location in the map layer is considered to be either "high-risk" or "not high-risk". This is like a criminal trial where the defendant is adjudicated guilty or not guilty; there is no finding of innocence or anything in between. The same is true of binary-valued aggravating risk map layers in that no place is deemed "low risk". The focus of such risk map layers is on places that pose the greatest (highest) risk; all other places are simply deemed to have qualities about them that make them not the greatest (not highest) risk. When binary-valued risk map layers are produced with all aggravating risk factors, the high-risk places get a value of +1, and all other (not high-risk) places get a value of 0 (zero). If mitigating risk map layers are used, the lowest-risk places get a value of -1, and all other (not lowest-risk) places get a value of 0 (zero). In a binary-valued risk map layer, every place either is or is not something: its density value is above +2 standard deviations from the mean (high-risk) or it isn't (not high-risk); its distance is less than 500 feet from an ATM (high-risk) or it isn't (not high-risk); it intersects with a street (high-risk) or it doesn't (not high-risk).

Colors, etc. are not important when operationalizing risk map layers. What matters is how places within your study area are classified and grouped according to the place-based influence of each particular risk factor. Essentially, this step of RTM constitutes a weighing (or indexing) procedure whereby every place within a map layer is assigned a value that represents that place's relationship to the risk factor and that place's influence on the outcome event. This indexing must be done in a way that is consistent with your operational definition of the risk factor, and it must be done similarly across all map layers. For example, if a binary-valued risk map layer is to be used for one risk factor, it should also be used for all other risk factors, or else comparisons across risk map layers will not be relative.

That is, for the most reliable and valid results, each risk factor should be operationalized in a consistent way across all risk map layers. For example, if risk factor "A" is operationalized in a dichotomous way (i.e. the risk is either present of absent), then your risk values might be 1 (risk is present) or 0 (risk is absent). In this case, 1 is the highest risk and 0 is the lowest risk. But, if risk factor "B" is operationalized as "the risk decreases with distance at intervals of 500ft" (i.e., distance from an ATM), then you might have risk values for that risk map layer of 3 (highest risk; within 500ft), 2 (medium risk; 501-1000ft), 1 (lower risk; 1001-1500ft), 0 (lowest risk; 1501ft and farther). Conceivably, these risk values could continue to negative infinity. If these two risk layers (A and B) were added together without any conversion to standardize their numbers, then a value of "1" within the risk map layer for factor A would be considered equal to the value of 1 within the risk map layer of factor B. This is not true. In fact, according to the operationalization of risk factor B, a value of 1 actually signifies "lower" risk. As you can see from this example, somehow you need to standardize the values within every risk map layer so that the numerical value of the place designated as the "highest risk" in one map layer is (relatively) equal to the numerical value of the place designated as the "highest risk" in all other map layers—regardless of how they were operationalized. Decide upon an indexing scheme for operationalizing risk factors early on, and use it for creating all risk map layers.

The next task to operationalizing risk map layers is to permanently assign risk values to cells. Symbology is only a temporary method of classifying raster cell values. It serves as preparation for the "Reclassify" operation, which assigns new, permanent values to each cell in a raster risk map layer. Use "Reclassify" in the Spatial Analyst Extension to permanently assign new attribute values to each raster cell according to how it was (temporarily) classified with symbology [On the "Spatial Analyst" toolbar, click Spatial Analyst > Reclassify].

Recall from a few paragraphs above that the 'ATM risk map layer' "would be classified with two categories: 1) all cells within a distance of 500ft from the nearest

ATM, and 2) all cells greater than 500ft from an ATM." With the "Reclassify" operation in Spatial Analyst, we can permanently assign each cell in the category of "all cells within a distance of 500ft from the nearest ATM" with the attribute value of "1" (i.e. highest risk), and each cell in the category of "all cells greater than 500ft from an ATM" with the attribute value of "0" (i.e. not highest risk). Then, every place throughout the 'ATM risk map layer' would be designated as being either high risk or not. The "Reclassify" operation makes this designation permanent and in accordance with how the risk factors were operationalized to the cells in the risk map layers. In fact, it is the only way to make new permanent raster cell values, and, therefore, is a very important task before combining all risk map layers together to form a composite risk terrain map (in Step 9) .

To use the "Reclassify" function: In the "Input Raster" field of the "Reclassify" dialog box, select the risk map layer whose values you want to permanently change. ("Reclassify" actually creates a new raster layer, so the original risk map layer will not be altered). Notice how the "Old values" are grouped into the same classification schema that the map was symbolized in. By default, the "New values" are ordered numerically (e.g. from 1 to 4). As exemplified in Figure 6, all cells with old values between zero (0) and 1.8308733713175455e-007 will get a new value of 1, and so on. Manually enter new values for each category accordingly. For the purposes of RTM, new values must be numerical. Choose a name and location to save the "Output raster" and then click the "OK" button. A new raster map will be created: As exemplified in Figure 6, each cell will have a value of 1, 2, 3 or 4; The Attribute table of this new (Reclassified) risk map layer shows that 13,712 cells now have the value of "1", 1,267 cells have the value "2", and so on.

Figure 6

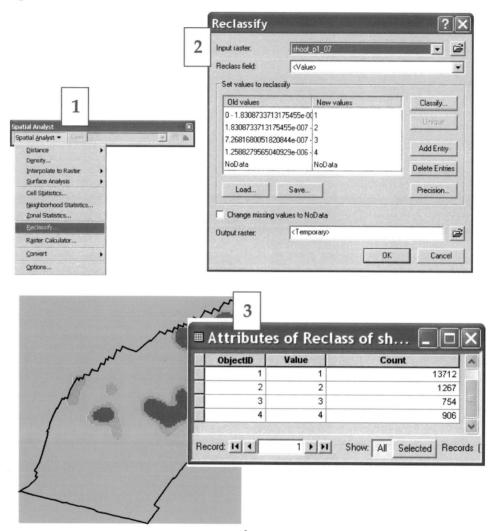

"NoData" Raster Cell Values: Make sure that you assign a value to the NoData cells. In a binary-valued risk map layer, for example, NoData will most likely receive the value of 0 (zero). NoData means that not enough information is known about a cell to assign it a value; or, that the cells are in areas that a user intentionally does not want to display (or wants to exclude from raster

calculations). NoData and 0 are not the same; 0 is a valid value. If NoData exists for any of the cells in a final risk map layer, that cell will not be included in the computation of the final composite risk values. This can jeopardize the validity and reliability of the risk terrain map. All "NoData" cells should be "Reclassified" with a neutral value, such as zero (0) in order to keep these cells in the equation.

Possible Error Message: You might receive an error message similar to the screen capture below when attempting to reclassify an input raster map in ArcGIS.

This message is likely related to a problem with the file directory path where your input raster layer is stored. To prevent this error, it is very important that all raster layers (and vector shapefiles) be stored on your computer to a directory path that does not have any spaces, dashes, periods, or other punctuation. For example, a common error (because of the spaces in the directory path) is to store raster layers to a directory such as "C:/Documents and Settings/User". These spaces between "Documents and Settings" make it so that ArcGIS is "Unable to initialize reclass table", as stated in the error message. To prevent this error, store all raster layers to directory paths without spaces from the onset of producing risk map layers and risk terrain maps. If you already saved raster layers to directories that might pose a problem, do not simply move (i.e. copy and paste) those existing raster layers to a new directory or change the path or directory name where the layers reside—it won't solve the problem. Instead, you must add the existing layer(s) to ArcMap, then right click on the layer in the Table of Contents and export it to a new directory. This creates a completely new layer and ensures that all references to it in the file's code point to the new, correct, directory path.

> *Decide upon an indexing scheme for operationalizing risk factors early on, and use it for creating all risk map layers.*

STEP 8: *Inter Risk Map Layer Weighting*

There are two types of weighting that can be done in risk terrain modeling. The first is somewhat inherent in the task of Step 7—when you operationalize every risk factor to a risk map layer and then "Reclassify" the cells according to a standard index, such as 0 or 1, negative 1 to positive 1, or 0 to +3. In this way, the influence of the risk factor is "weighed" about the geography. The second type of weighting weights the risk map layers relative to one another so that the most "important" risk factor affects the risk terrain map more so than the other risk factors.

For example, imagine that you have three risk map layers for the outcome event of bicycle theft: 1) poorly lighted areas, 2) high density of bike racks, and 3) obstructive shrubbery. All of these factors together in the same place might increase the likelihood of a bicycle theft occurring there, but places with a "high density of bike racks" should carry more weight because that's where the item to be stolen is usually located—the other factors just make the theft easier because it is more covert. Perhaps places in the "high density of bike racks" risk map layer should be deemed twice as risky for bicycle theft compared to both of the other risk factors. Then in this (simple and hypothetical) example, you would multiply the values of all cells in the 'bike rack risk map layer' by 2, and leave all other risk maps layers as is. Although all risk map layers were operationalized with binary values (i.e. 0 or 1), the 'bike racks risk map layer' would now carry more weight—and implies higher risk—than the other risk map layers.

Risk terrain models are considered "weighted" when the risk map layers are weighted relative to one another. Risk terrain models are considered "un-weighted" when risk map layers are operationalized according to a standard index (which is a must, as discussed above in Step 7) and when the influence of each risk map layer on the outcome event is considered to be equal, so relative weights are not assigned.

To weight risk map layers in a risk terrain model with some statistical rigor, we recommend using logistic regression analysis to identify the relative correlations of each risk factor on the outcome event. For example, imagine a risk terrain model for shootings in which you operationalized three risk factors as three separate risk map layers. (To calculate weights for these risk map layers, you will also need to make a point map of all the shooting incident locations). Create all four (the outcome event included) of these map layers using data from the time period that you selected in Step 3; they should all be in vector format. If the risk map layers are not vector (they are probably raster since converting everything to raster was part of Step 7), then use the "Convert raster to features" function in the Spatial Analyst Extension so that each raster cell is represented in a vector shapefile by its centroid point [in the "Output geometry type" field of the "Raster to Features" dialog box, select "Point" from the dropdown menu]. This point (i.e., risk factor point) should have only one attribute value; that is, the (risk) value that was operationalized/assigned to it in Step 7. (Vector data is necessary here because soon you will have to perform spatial joins, which cannot be done with raster data).

Create a blank vector grid of cells that covers your entire study (herein referred to as the "blank vector grid"). (The "Create Vector Grid Tool" in Hawth's Analysis Tools for ArcGIS is a convenient way to do this: www.spatialecology.com/htools/createvectorgrid.php; or use your own method). Make sure that the cell sizes of this blank vector grid are the same size that was used for your raster risk map layers. In our example for Step 8 there would now be five vector shapefiles: a blank vector grid of cells, points of shooting incidents, and a uniform grid of points for each of the three risk map layers. Now the objective is to assign four new attributes to cells in the "blank vector grid"; each attribute will be the value of the point that represents the cell of each risk map layer at that location, respectively. This can be done with a series of "Spatial Joins", each of which assigns attributes of the points to the cells in the blank vector grid. At the end of this process of spatial joins, there should be a vector grid of cells with at least four new attributes (i.e. columns) in the attribute table— one attribute specifying the count of shootings in that cell, and three other attributes specifying the (risk) value of each point that intersects that cell—one for each of the three risk map layers, respectively (See the screen captures in Chapter 7 for an example of spatially joined data). Finally, add a new field to the attribute table that will specify the presence or absence of a shooting in each cell (i.e., IF shooting count equals zero, THEN shootings are absent; IF shooting count is one or more, THEN shootings are present).

Export the attribute table of the final vector grid of cells (with all of the new attributes) as a DBF file [From the Attributes Table > click the "Options" button > Export...] and import it into a software application that can perform Logistic Regression analysis, such as SPSS. (To learn more about Logistic Regression analysis, see: http://faculty.chass.ncsu.edu/garson/PA765/logistic.htm   or http://www.ats.ucla.edu/stat/spss/dae/logit.htm). Create a regression model where each risk map layer is represented by its respective variable (i.e. attribute in the vector grid of cells), and the dependent variable is "Any Shooting (Yes/No)". The unit of analysis is cells within your study area (i.e. places are cells, and each row in the table represents one cell). So the statistical output will tell you the effect that each risk factor has on the likelihood of an outcome event happening in cells with that risk factor, when controlling for all other risk factors. Specifically, the Beta Coefficient (B) in the regression analysis output is the "weight" for each risk factor: multiply that value to all cell values in its respective risk map layer. Then return to ArcMap and use the "Reclassify" tool in the Spatial Analyst Extension to change the old raster values of each risk map layer to the new weighted risk values that you calculated.

STEP 9: Combine Risk Map Layers to Form a Composite Map.

Use the Raster Calculator in the Spatial Analyst Extension to add all (weighted or un-weighted) raster risk map layers together to produce a composite map [From the "Spatial Analyst" toolbar, click "Spatial Analyst" > Raster Calculator]. The "Raster Calculator" operation creates a new raster map whereby the value of each cell is computed by applying map algebra to the value of the cells on one or more existing (raster) risk map layers. Essentially, it produces a new composite map. Consider, for example, the two raster layers shown in Figure 7. In each layer, cell values range from 0 to 2. If "Raster Calculator" were to be used to add each cell's values on these two layers, the result would be a composite raster map with cell values (potentially) ranging from 0 to 4.

The "Raster Calculator" dialog box provides for building algebra-like expressions that will produce new maps. Variables (in the form of raster layers and/or numbers) and functions are inserted into the expression box either by typing, by double-clicking on the layer names in the "Layers" section, or by using the buttons. Once an expression has been fully specified, click the "Evaluate" button to generate a new raster map. Congratulations, this is your risk terrain map!

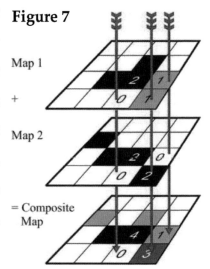

Figure 7

Map 1

+

Map 2

= Composite Map

STEP 10: Finalize the Risk Terrain Map to Communicate Meaningful Information.

The resulting composite map from the "Raster Calculator" operation (in Step 9) is your risk terrain map. Symbolize this map in a meaningful way so that it clearly communicates information about the study area for purposes of strategic decision-making and/or tactical action [From ArcMap's Table of Contents, right-click the (risk terrain map's) layer > Properties > "Symbology" tab]. Symbolizing raster map layers differs slightly from vector maps. When trying to change the symbology, you may get a message that says "Unique histogram does not exist. Do you want to compute unique values?" Click "Yes". In the "Layer Properties" dialog box, under the "Symbology" tab, click the "Classify" button under the "Classified" scheme (on the left). Standard Deviation is a good option for showing variation in raster values, especially risk terrain maps.

Your choice of symbology and classification schemes might imply areas that some people would call "hotspots" or clusters of high-risk upon visual inspection alone. However, this terminology should be used cautiously. The (often) arbitrary choice of colors and classification ranges, or the classification method (e.g. Equal Interval, Natural Breaks, Standard Deviation) could substantially change a map's appearance. For this reason, a cluster of high-risk places defined upon visual inspection is much different than a "statistically significant" cluster.

To be statistically significant, a group of cells must have high values and be surrounded by other cells with high values. Similarly, clusters of low-risk places consist of cells with low values surrounded by other cells with low values. This pattern must occur beyond random chance. The "Hotspot Analysis" tool in ArcGIS calculates the Getis-Ord Gi* statistic (Z score) for each feature in a dataset. The larger the statistically significant positive Z score is, the more intense the clustering of high values. The smaller the statistically significant negative Z score is, the more intense the clustering of low values. You can use the "Hotspot Analysis" tool to create a final map that shows clusters of places in your study area that are high-risk or low-risk. Or, as already discussed in Chapter 2, the "Cluster and Outlier Analysis" tool in ArcGIS might be preferred because it can identify clusters of places with values similar in magnitude as well as features that are spatial outliers. For example, whereas the resultant Z score from the Getis-Ord Gi* statistic can only tell where features with either high or low values cluster spatially surrounded by other similarly-valued features, the "Cluster and Outlier Analysis" tool can distinguish between statistically significant clusters of high values surrounded high values (HH), low values surrounded by low values (LL), high values surrounded by low values (HL), and low values surrounded by high values (LH). (Note that you must convert the risk terrain map into a grid of vector polygons in order to use the hotspot or cluster analysis tools. Use the "Convert Raster Cells to Vector Polygon Grid" Tool in the

RTM Toolbox to perform the vector conversion in a way that maintains each cell's composite risk value). For both of these aforementioned cluster or hotspot analysis tools, the field containing the composite risk values is your analysis field.

NOTE: ArcGIS Desktop Help presents "3 things to consider when undertaking any hotspot analysis". You should review this help section by searching for keywords "How hotspot analysis works" > click to view the first topic found.

To clip the risk terrain map (e.g., to your city's borders) you need to use a raster clipping tool. This can be found in ArcToolbox under Data Management Tools > Raster > Raster Processing. You can also find vector and raster clipping tools by searching for keyword "clip" in the Search tab of ArcToolbox. Double-clicking on the tool in the results area opens it directly.

CHAPTER SIX
TESTING THE STATISTICAL VALIDITY OF YOUR RISK TERRAIN MODEL

Testing the predictive validity of your risk terrain model is optional. The advantage of doing so is that it gives your model empirical credibility and allows for the estimation of future events with a certain degree of confidence. The drawback is that it requires outcome event data from the subsequent time period of your risk terrain model data. So for example, if your risk terrain map was produced with data from January through June, you would need outcome event data from July through December in order to test the six-month predictive validity. You could assume that your model is valid (which the technical steps above should help to make it so), and then validate your model after it has been used and the subsequent time period has ended. Or, you could produce a risk terrain map using data from two periods back to test your model's predictive validity with current outcome event data and then, if found to be valid, replicate the risk terrain model using current risk factor data to forecast the subsequent time period.

The procedure for testing a risk terrain model's validity can also be used to compare which time period a model is best able to forecast for. For example, existing research has shown that risk terrain models from January through June can forecast locations of shootings during July through December with statistical validity[63]. However, your tests might show that, in fact, the "January through June" model is a stronger predictor of locations of outcome events during the same time period the following year.

That is, for instance, "January through June 2010" could be a better predictor of "January through June 2011" than "July through December 2010". Or, you might find that time periods work best when they are in weekly, monthly, quarterly, yearly, etc. intervals. The best model will likely differ across different settings, extents, and jurisdictions; what works best for the NJ State Police might not work best for the L.A. County Sheriff, for instance.

We recommend using regression analysis to test the validity of your risk terrain model. There are many ways in which to do this, including a Logistic Regression or Ordinary Least Squares Regression; and there are many tools to use, including external software like SPSS or GeoDa, or the "Ordinary Least Square" or "Geographically Weighted Regression" tools in ArcMap. It is beyond the scope of this manual to direct you to one particular method since there are many legitimate methods and because it requires at least an intermediate level of statistical knowledge that is somewhat specific to the method used. Here, we will discuss the steps that will probably be required to prepare the risk terrain map and outcome event data for statistical testing. We will also discuss some important considerations that should be had when performing the tests.

Ultimately, you will need an attributes table of the risk terrain map of your study area with at least two variables: (1) composite risk value of each cell and (2) count of outcome events (e.g. shooting incidents) for each cell. Raster data do not permit more than one attribute value per cell, so you will need to convert your (raster) risk terrain map to a vector grid of cells. You can do this using the "Convert Raster Cells to Vector Polygon Grid" tool in the RTM Toolbox in a way that maintains the integrity of each cell (you need each raster cell to be a unique polygon feature in the vector-ized risk terrain map). With a vector risk terrain map, you may use a "Spatial Join" to get a count of shooting points in each cell. In the screen capture below, the risk terrain map from the Irvington,

NJ example in Chapter 3 was converted to vector polygons and then joined with geocoded shooting points to yield the two attribute variables needed to perform statistical tests. The attribute table can be exported as a DBF and imported into a statistical software package.

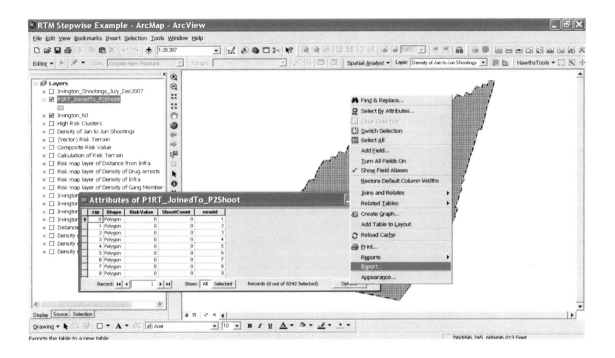

Keep in mind that spatial autocorrelation might exist for your outcome event, which would need to be controlled for in a regression model. Distributions among geographical units, such as grid cells, are usually not independent, meaning that values found in a particular cell are likely to be influenced by corresponding values in nearby cells[64]. Moran's I measures this autocorrelation, with values approaching 1 when geographical units are situated near other similar geographical units, and approaching – 1 when geographical units are situated near dissimilar geographical units. A Moran's I value of 0 indicates the absence of autocorrelation, or independence, among geographical units. GeoDa, a freestanding software application, can be used to calculate

Moran's I values for each risk terrain with a Queen Contiguity Weight matrix[65]. ArcMap also has a "Spatial Autocorrelation (Moran's I)" tool that can be used. If spatial autocorrelation is found to be statistically significant, calculate a spatial lag variable for each cell (via tools in GeoDa or the "Generate Spatial Weights Matrix" tool in ArcMap) and include that variable in your regression model as a control.

Crime incidents are oftentimes located by street addresses in police datasets. Therefore, their exact locations are usually unknown beyond the street name and number that was assigned to each incident. For example, if a shooting occurred in a back yard that was several hundred meters from the street in front of the house, the location of the shooting would nonetheless be recorded as the dwelling's street address. This is common practice for most police departments. However, for the purpose of testing risk terrain models with real data, your risk terrain map should match the limitations of administrative police records of outcome events by assuming that shootings (as in this example) can only occur on streets to which the data was geocoded. In other words, a risk terrain map that is truly representative of the outcome event locations that it is forecasting should only include cells that intersect with streets if the events are recorded by street address. Strictly according to the way in which the data is collected, all other places in the study area could not have a shooting incident. This is of course a moot point if outcome event locations are recorded precisely, such as with GPS devices and XY coordinates.

For visual presentations a full map of the study area looks best and it shows all places that could conceivably have an outcome event happen—even if the incident is recorded to the closest street address. But including all cells could bias the results of statistical tests because cells would be included where it would be impossible for a crime to happen according to the way in which locations are recorded in the dataset. To address this issue, create a new risk terrain map that includes only cells that intersect with streets. As shown in the screen capture below, "Select by Spatial Location" (all cells that intersect with streets) was used to prepare a risk terrain map that was used for statistical testing. Once the cells that intersect with streets are selected, they can be exported to create a new map layer. In this example, there were 8,242 100'x100' cells that comprised the original risk terrain map; 3,990 100'x100' cells now comprise the "street intersected" map. All of the cells in the "street intersected" map could conceivably have a shooting recorded within it. These cells serve as the unit of analysis for subsequent statistical tests.

The procedure for testing a risk terrain model's validity can also be used to determine which time period a model is best able to forecast for.

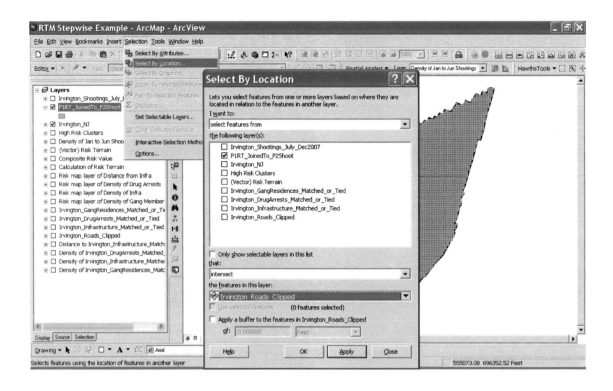

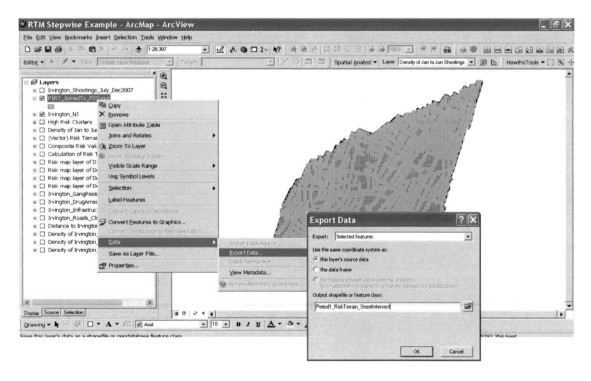

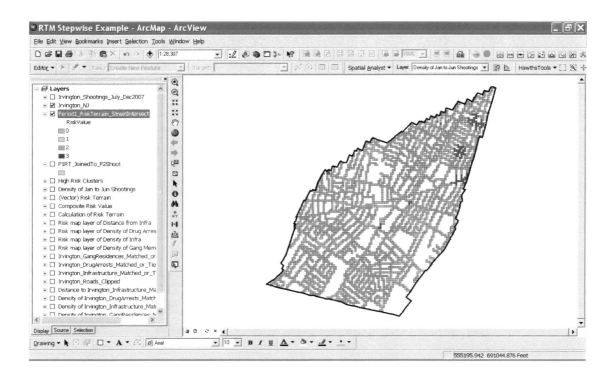

RTM accurately forecasts new crimes at specific places that are meaningful to police and manageable for targeted interventions.

Upon visual analysis of the map, police commanders might direct patrols to clusters of streets with high risk for shootings as a traditional form of deterrence.

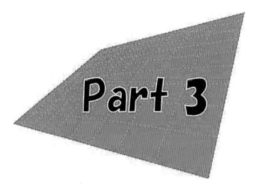

Part 3

Concluding Comments and Caveats

CHAPTER SEVEN
RISK TERRAIN MAPS AS SPATIAL INTELLIGENCE

Risk Reduction vs. Response to Crisis

Police have an important role to play in affecting the risk of crime within an area. They can deter offenders, embolden victims, and harden targets. These actions can have the overall impact of reducing crime occurrence, but we need to separate what we see as risk reduction strategies from prevention and response activities. The risk reduction approach suggests that we choose one or more factors from the risk terrain model to propose strategies that mitigate the factors' impact, interrupt the interactions that lead to crime outcomes, and ultimately reduce overall risk. Prevention strategies, instead, operate on the basis of responding to crime occurrence, targeting areas based on what has happened previously as a way of suggesting that if it happened in this location once, it will happen there again. Our tests of risk terrain models that forecast on the basis of certain place-based factors have produced results suggesting that contextual models are more accurate in forecasting future crime than are models based solely on previous crime occurrences (see Chapter 2).

We argue, then, that risk terrain modeling must be incorporated into a policing strategy that allocates resources (and deploys interventions) in a proactive rather than reactive manner. This might involve the incorporation of risk terrain maps into existing CompStat programs to consider what the high-risk areas are based on reasoned analysis of key factors that interact in space and time to form certain types of crime-prone locations. Top commanders (such as those present at CompStat meeting) and/or patrol officers could provide valuable insight into place-based factors that can be modeled in risk terrains maps of certain types of crimes. Their input and interaction with RTM will give risk terrain maps and the intelligence derived from them added credibility, and help to ensure meaningful and actionable information. The RTM approach gives crime analysts a new conceptual framework to develop innovative ways for police agencies to combat safety and security issues in their jurisdictions.

The flexibility of risk terrain modeling methods and the extents to which they can be applied would allow police to strategically incorporate known areas of concern in their assessment of locations that might generate violence—a practical reality suggested by Ratcliffe and McCullagh[66]. Then police could assign resources accordingly to address one or more of the factors in the risk terrain model at the regional and/or local levels. For example, they might institute community policing strategies that engage other municipal agencies and address problems of social disorganization, including the strict enforcement of ordinances related to vacant properties; public works departments might be instructed to limit roadway access to troubled areas, such as drug markets; and, parole officers might be consulted to better evaluate reentry plans of incarcerated offenders who will return to high-risk areas. As these examples suggest, risk terrain modeling has the potential to enhance short- and long-term strategic decision-making activities regarding such things as tactical operations, case management, and resource allocation. RTM can also be particularly valuable to police agencies when fiscal budgets are tight because they do not require new or exceedingly great investments in hardware or software. They only require a dynamic way of thinking about crime problems, their causes, and situational impacts of police interventions.

Risk Terrain Modeling in ACTION

If we see policing as a process of risk management, risk terrain modeling is a tool that can be used in the application of intelligence-based policing. In their discussion of risk, Kennedy and Van Brunschot[67] introduced the idea of the ACTION model as offering a framework by which police organizations can embed evidence-based analysis of risk into their organizations (see Figure 8). The risk terrain modeling approach to spatial risk assessment facilitates this framework and incorporates or permits all three of its key elements: risk assessment, risk management, and risk governance. Underlying these elements is the basic view that agencies engaged in improving the effectiveness of their activities must incorporate risk-based intelligence in a way that promotes proactive planning rather than reactive programs.

Risk terrain modeling allows for the articulation of what we know about crime causes, and it does so at a unit of analysis that police are operationally conditioned for—geographic places. The ACTION model provides ways of understanding and responding to high-risk places based on sound conceptual thinking; encourages evaluation as a key element in judging success; and promotes notifying others in the organization and the community of its outcomes. When used together, RTM and the ACTION model can facilitate comprehensive understandings of crime problems, smooth flows of information, and permit efficient allocations of resources. Most likely, certain elements of the ACTION model will be used for developing risk terrain models.

> *Risk terrain modeling allows for the articulation of what we know about crime causes, and it does so at a unit of analysis that police are operationally conditioned for—the geography.*

Figure 8	
A	Assessing Vulnerabilities, Exposure and Threats
C	Making Connections
T	Setting Tasks to Respond and Prevent
I	Collecting Information about Events
O	Refining the Organization
N	Notifying Others

A key element in forecasting crime is taking account of what we know and what we don't know about people and places. Spatial risk assessment addresses certain vulnerabilities of places, but it also draws attention to uncertainty regarding the dynamic interaction of these places and the people who travel or reside there. In developing a risk terrain model, you should attempt to reduce uncertainty through a detailed understanding of the qualities of micro-level places within the larger communities under study and the threats that certain features pose to individuals and social order. The uncertainty inherent in studying the social and environmental "fabric" of communities can be minimized by collecting and using valid and reliable data from a variety of sources. Especially sources beyond (traditional) police statistics.

The most accurate *assessments* of environmental vulnerabilities and criminal threats require data that is not reliant on police activities. For example, a heavy reliance on crime incident or arrest data can make spatial risk assessment difficult as it presumes that all offenders who pose threats are eventually arrested, and that future arrests or incidents will occur in the same places. Clearly this is not the case. At a minimum, though, we might presume that arrested individuals represent a cross-section of those who might be offenders and that the places where their crimes occurred might be chronically criminogenic. This supposition reduces some uncertainty because it improves our knowledge about likely criminogenic places. But, it does not explain why these places are criminogenic; that is, what risk factors present at those areas make them attractive for crime? When developing a risk terrain model, strive to account for characteristics of places beyond the known offenders who frequent them or the crimes that already occurred there. For instance, violent incidents might be symptomatic of something like market demand for drugs in certain places, or the resistance that comes from residents against allowing street crime to continue. Understanding the qualities of places that are ideal for selling drugs and then mapping these qualities as risk map layers would be a much better articulation of an area's criminogenic risk than only knowledge about crime incidents that already happened there.

The risk terrain modeling approach can identify vulnerable (i.e. high-risk) places by connecting elements of the social and physical character of those areas. Police scholars know from extensive research that these elements matter in crime but they are not routinely included in forecasts of crime emergence and distribution. RTM provides a means to do this as part of a risk assessment process that connects activities of individuals and groups within the physical contexts of their environments. This helps to anticipate how these and other people might pattern their behaviors over time. One example of this is to ask patrol officers and detectives about social networks in certain areas. This could go a long way to reduce the uncertainty about who is involved in crime and how their activities might be influenced by the geography. Certain geographic influences (e.g. "Clique A has their 'meetings' at fire hydrants") could be made into a risk map layer for the entire jurisdiction (e.g. 'fire hydrant risk map layer'), and then included in a risk terrain model. By drawing from the experiences of individuals who patrol an area and who are in constant contact with individuals living there, analysts can increase their understanding of what is going on where, and what qualities of spaces might be attracting offenders and generating crime. Importantly, data about these risk factors must be collated and made available to analysts involved in risk terrain modeling, even if they are traditionally not "police data".

Police reports, victim surveys, or other textual (qualitative) information could also be studied quickly with text analysis programs (such as QDA-Miner; www.provalisresearch.com) to locate important clues about immediate precursors to reported crime incidents or how problems developed over time and resulted in crime at certain places. For example, a long time resident of the city, but recent crime victim filing a report, might explain (or vent) to police that the physical decline in her neighborhood over many years provides an ideal environment for illicit activities; i.e., vacant houses with no clearly identified occupants became havens for drug dealers and users. Police might use this information immediately to deter outsiders from traveling to certain places—possibly to obtain drugs; Analysts might use this information to recognize the value of "vacant properties" as a risk factor for drug-related crimes and include it in a risk terrain model. Information from incident reports may also provide insight into how offenders themselves can be operationalized as risk factors for certain types of crimes. For example, mapping the relative locations of where offenders and their victims lived could establish the extent to which living in proximity to offenders puts victims at risk. A risk map layer could then be created to note places within a certain distance from (e.g. sex) offenders' residences.

There are good tools now available to analysts to do physical audits of environments in a systematic and time efficient way, such as with the street view setting of Google Maps (www.google.com/maps). Start, for example, by virtually touring places with known hotspots and coldspots of crime to see if unique characteristics of each environment can be identified. As exemplified in the screen capture below, if hotspots of certain types of crime are characterized as having the ability to fortify houses that serve as locations to stash drugs, then this information might serve as a risk map layer. If not included in a risk terrain model, this information could at least provide context for interpreting risk terrain maps. Consider using Google Maps and other public and open-source technologies to determine where vacant properties are, how streets are lighted, and so on to reduce uncertainty and enhance the validity of your risk terrain model.

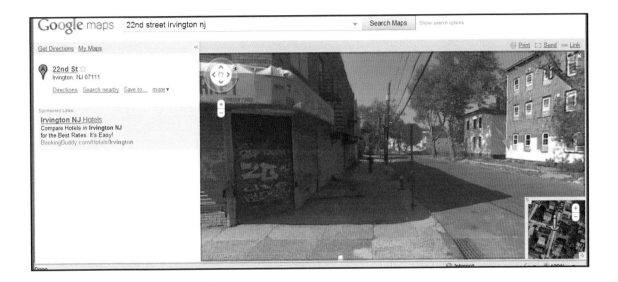

You might also consider the costs of crime on the community as risk factors in a risk terrain model because, as costs mount, they become signs or symptoms of vulnerable areas that may be more conducive to future crime. These costs may be hard to measure in real dollar terms, but there are other ways including the change in neighborhood infrastructure (i.e. increased vacancy rates, declining average incomes, and so on; e.g., see screen capture from Zillow.com below); changes in insurance premiums or the degree to which people can insure their homes or cars; or added costs to the township that come from repairs of infrastructure or necessary security measures at schools. These signs or symptoms of growing crime problems are not always easily operationalized as risk map layers, but there is enough solid research[68] to show that areas that suffer in these ways are also confounded by problems of crime and violence.

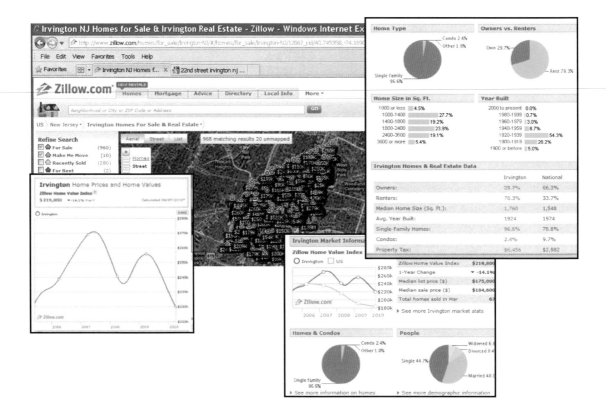

An important part of risk assessment—especially for the purpose of developing interventions, relates to the identification of key players in certain places and their likely involvement in crime. For example, the drug trade contains certain individuals who assume control and may lead others to violence in maintaining territory. Understanding who these individuals are and who their rivals are, can go a long way to control certain crimes. As an example of this, there was a story of two gang members (who were brothers) who were thought to be influential in the drug trade in a local neighborhood of a major city. These two had been arrested before for violent crimes and had active arrest warrants related to selling drugs. At the same time, a major rival was about to be released from prison and the worry on the part of the police was that, once free, the rival would seek to "take out" his opponents and reclaim the drug market for himself. The police moved quickly to reduce this risk (in a known and specific location) by serving the warrants on the two brothers so that, in the short term at least, violence would be avoided and more strategic long-term risk reduction strategies could be implemented.

Addressing vulnerabilities at high-risk places means focusing on the extent to which you can do something about reducing the likelihood that crime will occur by mitigating one or more of the risk factors included in the risk terrain model. If there are certain known targets of crime, can they be protected or removed? Can offenders be deterred? If there are places that are ideal for certain types of criminal activity can they be altered to make them less attractive to criminals? Can police restrict movement into and out of high-risk areas to interrupt the flow of offenders (i.e. drug dealers and buyers) and victims (people who may be innocent bystanders who get attacked for money or for reasons of territorial control)?

When interpreting risk terrain maps, pay close attention to the situations that unfold in high-risk places (including a clear understanding that risk is not constant across time or place but can vary by time of day or day of the week or can move from one location to another in response to law enforcement pressure). The situational prevention ideas that form interventions to mitigate risks should address how police might alter vulnerabilities of places and the people and properties within them.

Vulnerability at high risk places must also be considered in the context of how far along the damage is that has been done to the social and physical infrastructure of a community when the intervention begins. If streets are poorly lit, if the schools are in disarray, or if the parks are unsafe, this means that the risks of crime are higher and the likelihood of success in introducing situational prevention strategies is greatly reduced. Understanding long-standing risk factors (even if your risk terrain model is comprised of data from a limited time period) is important for dealing with the high-risk places—there may be a form of self-fulfilling prophecy that develops in these areas which keeps the residents from engaging in self-help and makes policy makers and police more reluctant to invest greater resources into areas deemed "unsalvageable". This might very well be the greatest hurdle faced when beginning to mitigate risks in high-risk areas.

Risk terrain modeling allows police to make *connections* between risk factors, crimes, and the ways in which these factors are addressed at different places. Furthermore, RTM allows police to focus on opportunity reduction at high risk places rather than only focus on identifying and removing offenders from these places. For example, police might consider a more broad scale approach that includes dealing with the problems of social disorder, which might involve community activation programs (such as engaging the community in crime prevention plans) or neighborhood clean-up drives. Whatever is decided, the intervention should articulate the underlying assumptions that are being followed and guided by the data that comprises the risk terrain model.

Ethical Concerns in Using Risk Measures to Guide Interventions: The call for spatial risk assessments derives from a concern that police more clearly understand the total picture when taking action against crime. But, police need to be aware that risk assessments can become tools that can be used unfairly against certain groups that are seen as being highly dangerous. Risk terrain maps should not be offered as an excuse to put pressure on communities in a way that assumes that they will be troublesome, without providing alternatives and continued monitoring (or accountability) within the assessments of risk. The targeting of police interventions that emerge from risk terrain maps are based on a sound understanding of geographic attributes and qualities of space that connect to crime outcomes. Risk terrain maps do not identify individuals from specific groups or characteristics of people as likely candidates for crime—a tactic that has led police agencies to be accused of profiling. Nevertheless, care must be taken in police departments to reinforce the idea that people who make risk terrain maps should be accountable to certain standards. Without this, mistakes can be made that will be a problem for future initiatives.

Furthermore, police organizations have an obligation to explain to their constituents that they identify and deal with risks faced within their jurisdictions, as well as communicating the steps that are being taken to mitigate these risks. Obviously, the conversation around risk will be affected by fear and may lead to demands that are hard to meet or not realistic given the risk factors that exist. But with the help of a clearly stated risk terrain model and comprehensive (interdisciplinary, multi-agency) plans to mitigate risk factors, these fears may be directly addressed and managed. Risk terrain maps may be used to communicate priority places for interventions and/or the steps that are being taken to address risks. The complexities of risk terrain modeling and risk management strategies may not fit into the day-to-day accounts of crime statistics. But the advantage of having clearly informed decisions that back up responses to the risks that have been documented could go a long way to provide context in which the public (and the media) can judge the likelihood of success of an intervention and the long term prospects for the problems faced in neighborhoods.

Working with other agencies in high-risk locations (including probation and parole officers, school officials, and community groups) allows a better coordination of response and clear definition of *tasks*. There have been a number of efforts at this type of reaction (ranging from Neighborhood Watch programs to more specific violence intervention programs, such as Operation Ceasefire). These programs are based on certain assumptions about how crime occurs and can be stopped but, as importantly, they provide a clear set of guidelines concerning who should do what in prevention and response. This task assignment is a key element in any risk management (i.e. intervention) program that is implemented.

Also key to successful completion of a risk management plan is a well-organized information system that provides reliable data about outcome events and permits an ongoing evaluation of the success of the intervention. It is sometimes difficult to collect detailed *information* about police movements and intervention impacts beyond incident or arrest data. However, with a clearly articulated set of goals defined in the intervention plan, the required data can be defined and efforts made to collect it. Risk terrain modeling allows for an iterative assessment of the environmental changes that can be attributed to the actions of police or other agencies over the time of their involvement in certain places to mitigate risks there. Analysts should take full advantage of the evaluation methods that RTM permits by encouraging the collection of valid and reliable measures of intervention impacts. This might include collaborating among multiple agencies by way of pooled data.

Risk governance using RTM requires that an *organization* shift its focus away from a truly reactive stance to one that is more proactive. In this way, it becomes a knowledge-based enterprise that relies on information about its current functioning and its environment to set goals, to evaluate actions, and to plan its resources. The primary intention for using a risk terrain modeling approach is to mitigate and reduce risk at certain places. That is, to respond to crimes as they happen and also to be responsive to risky places as they become known. This may not be too hard to do given the new receptivity to intelligence-led policing, but to truly make RTM an effective approach for crime analysts, the police leadership must begin to think in terms of risk factors and priorities and send a clear signal to the organization of the value of evidence-based decision-making in planning risk abatement strategies. Police must be proactive in *notifying* others within the organization about the program of assessment and the connections that are made. In addition, involving the community in risk reduction strategies is a vital part of success in police operations. Once this shift occurs, risk terrain modeling can become a tool to perpetuate risk-based intelligence-led policing. Or perhaps the analytical framework of RTM will become the catalyst that initiates the long-desired shift to risk-based policing.

Importantly, RTM keeps the <u>analyst</u> in crime analysis, which is not a point-and-click occupation to be replaced by expensive software or hardware upgrades. Crime analysis requires thoughtful questions, theoretical grounding, and meaningful interpretations and communication of results by experts with technical know-how and insights from the field. RTM is a tool for this endeavor.

The risk terrain modeling approach can identify vulnerable places by connecting elements of the social and physical character of those areas.

The flexibility of risk terrain modeling methods and the extents to which they can be applied allow police to strategically incorporate known areas of concern in their assessments of locations that might generate crime.

Endnotes

[1] Sacco, V. F. & Kennedy, L. W. (2002). *The Criminal Event: Perspectives in Space and Time, Second Edition* . Belmont, CA: Wadsworth.

[2] Kennedy, L. W. & Van Brunschot, E. G. (2009). *The Risk in Crime*. New York: Roman and Littlefield.

[3] For example: Sherman, L. W, Gartin, P. R. & Buerger, M. E. (1989). Hot spots of predatory crime: Routine activities and the criminology of place. *Criminology. 27*: 821-849; Harries, K. (1999). Mapping Crime: Principles and Practice, National Hills, CA; Eck, J. E. (2001). Policing and crime event concentration. In Meier, R., Kennedy, L., & Sacco, V. (eds.), The process and structure of crime: Criminal events and crime analysis, Transactions, New Brunswick, NJ, pp. 249-276; Eck, J. E., Chainey, S., Cameron, J. G., Leitner, M., & Wilson, R. E. (2005). Mapping Crime: Understanding Hot Spots, National Institute of Justice. Washington, DC.

[4] Abbott, A. (1997). Of time and space: The contemporary relevance of the Chicago. *Social Forces. 75*: 1149-1182.

[5] Shevky, E. & Bell, W. (1955). *Social Area Analysis: Theory, Illustrative Application and Computational Procedures*. Stanford: Stanford University Press.

[6] Cohen, L. E., Kluegel, J., & Land, K. (1981). Social inequality and predatory criminal victimization: An exposition and test of formal theory. *American Sociological Review, 46*: 505-524.

[7] Eck, J. E. (2001). Policing and crime event concentration. In Meier, R., Kennedy, L., & Sacco, V. (eds.), The process and structure of crime: Criminal events and crime analysis, Transactions, New Brunswick, NJ, pp. 249-276; Eck, J. E. (2002). "Preventing crime at places." Pp. 241-294 in *Evidence-Based Crime Prevention*, edited by L. W. Sherman, D. P. Farrington, B. C. Welsh, and D. L. MacKenzie. New York: Routledge.

[8] Mears, D. P., Scott, M. L., & Bhati, A. S. (2007). Opportunity theory and agricultural crime victimization. *Rural Sociology, 72*; 151-184.

[9] Brantingham, P. & Brantingham, P. 1995. "Criminality of Place: Crime Generators and Crime Attractors." *European Journal on Criminal Policy and Research* 3:1-26.

[10] Kennedy, L. W. & Van Brunschot, E. G. (2009). *The Risk in Crime*. New York: Roman and Littlefield.

[11] Eck, J. E. & Weisburd, D. (1995). Crime and Place, Willow Tree Press, Mosney, NY.

[12] Block, R. L. & Block, C. R. (1995). Space, place & crime: Hot spot areas & hot places of liquor-related crime. In Eck, J.E. & Weisburd, D. (eds.), Crime and Place: Crime Prevention Studies (Vol. 4), Willow Tree Press, Monsey, NY, pp. 145-184.

[13] Brantingham, P. J., & Brantingham, P. L. (1981). *Environmental Criminology*. Sage. Beverly Hills.

[14] Brantingham, P. & Brantingham, P. 1995. Criminality of Place: Crime Generators and Crime Attractors. *European Journal on Criminal Policy and Research* 3:1-26.

[15] Eck, J. E. (1995). A general model of the geography of illicit retail marketplaces. In Eck, J. E. & Weisburd, D. (eds.), Crime and place: Crime Prevention Studies (Vol. 4), Willow Tree Press: Modney, NJ, pp. 67-95; Ritter, A. (2006). Studying illicit drug markets: Disciplinary contributions. *International Journal of Drug Policy. 17*: 453--463.

[16] Mazerolle, L., Kadleck, C., & Roehl, J. (2004). Differential police control at drug-dealing places. *Security Journal. 17*: 1-69; Eck, J. E. (1995). A general model of the geography of illicit retail marketplaces. In Eck, J. E. & Weisburd, D. (eds.), Crime and place: Crime Prevention Studies (Vol. 4), Willow Tree Press, Modney, NJ, pp. 67-95.

[17] Kennedy, L. W. & Van Brunschot, E. G. (2009). *The Risk in Crime*. New York: Roman and Littlefield.

[18] Kennedy, L. W. & Van Brunschot, E. G. (2009). *The Risk in Crime*. New York: Roman and Littlefield.

[19] For example, see: Brantingham, P. J., & Brantingham, P. L. (1981). *Environmental Criminology*. Sage. Beverly Hills.

[20] Sampson, R.J., S.W. Raudenbush, and F. Earls 1997 Neighborhoods and Violent Crime: A Multilevel Study of Collective Efficacy Science 277, 15: 918-924.

[21] Groff, E. R. 2007."'Situating' Simulation to Model Human Spatio-Temporal Interactions: An Example Using Crime Events." *Transactions in GIS*, 11(4):507-530; Groff, E. R. 2007. "Simulation for Theory Testing and Experimentation: An Example Using Routine Activity Theory and Street Robbery." *Journal of Quantitative Criminology* 23:75-103.

[22] Ratcliffe, J. H. & Rengert, G. F. (2008). Near repeat patterns in Philadelphia shootings, *Security Journal,* 21(1-2): 58-76.

[23] Ratcliffe, J. H. & Rengert, G. F. (2008). Near repeat patterns in Philadelphia shootings, *Security Journal,* 21(1-2): 58-76.

[24] Ratcliffe, J. H. & Rengert, G. F. (2008). Near repeat patterns in Philadelphia shootings, *Security Journal,* 21(1-2): p. 62; see also: Bowers, K. J. and Johnson, S. D. (2004) Who Commits Near Repeats? A Test of the Boost Explanation. *Western Criminology Review*. Vol. 5, No. 3, pp 12 – 24; Johnson, S. D. and Bowers, K. J. (2004a) The Burglary as Clue to the Future: The Beginnings of Prospective Hot-Spotting. *European Journal of Criminology*. Vol. 1, pp 237 – 255; Johnson, S. D. and Bowers, K. J. (2004b) The Stability of Space – Time Clusters of Burglary. *British Journal of Criminology*. Vol. 44, No. 1, pp 55 – 65.

[25] see Kennedy, L. W. & Forde, D., (1999). When Push Comes to Shove: A Routine Conflict Approach to Violence. Albany: SUNY Press.

[26] http://www.jratcliffe.net/papers/Ratcliffe%20(2003)%20Intelligence%20led%20policing.pdf; Ratcliffe, JH (2003, April) Intelligence led policing. *Trends and Issues in Crime and Criminal Justice*, Paper 248.

27 http://www.jratcliffe.net/papers/Ratcliffe%20(2003)%20Intelligence%20led%20policing.pdf; Ratcliffe, JH (2003, April) Intelligence led policing. *Trends and Issues in Crime and Criminal Justice*, Paper 248.

28 John, T. & Maguire, M. (2004). The National Intelligence Model: Key lessons from early research, Home Office; http://rds.homeoffice.gov.uk/rds/pdfs04/rdsolr3004.pdf

29 John, T. & Maguire, M. (2004). The National Intelligence Model: Key lessons from early research, Home Office; http://rds.homeoffice.gov.uk/rds/pdfs04/rdsolr3004.pdf

30 Maguire, M. (2000). Researching 'Street Criminal a Neglected Art, in king, R and Wincup, (eds.)Doing Research on Crime and Justice, Oxford: Oxford University Press; Maguire, M and T. John. 2006. "Intelligence Led Policing, Managerialism and Community Engagement: Competing Priorities and the Roles of the National Intelligence Model in the UK." Policing and Society 16: 67-85.

31 Maguire, M. (2000). Researching 'Street Criminal a Neglected Art, in king, R and Wincup, (eds.)Doing Research on Crime and Justice, Oxford: Oxford University Press. Pp. 326; Maguire, M and T. John. 2006. "Intelligence Led Policing, Managerialism and Community Engagement: Competing Priorities and the Roles of the National Intelligence Model in the UK." Policing and Society 16: 67-85.

32 Maguire, M and T. John. 2006. "Intelligence Led Policing, Managerialism and Community Engagement: Competing Priorities and the Roles of the National Intelligence Model in the UK." Policing and Society 16: 67-85.

33 Van Brunschot, E. & Kennedy, L. W. (2008). *Risk Balance and Security*. Thousand Oaks, CA: Sage Publications.

34 Innes, M. N. Fielding and N. Cope (2005) "The appliance of science: the theory and practice of crime intelligence analysis", British Journal of Criminology. (45/1) pp.39-57 [p. 42]

35 Sacco, V. F. & Kennedy, L. W. (2002). *The Criminal Event: Perspectives in Space and Time, Second Edition* . Belmont, CA: Wadsworth.

36 Tomlin, C. D. (1994). Map algebra: One perspective. *Landscape and Urban Planning, 30*, 3–12.

37 Risk Terrain Modeling (RTM) is similar to the approach adopted by Groff and La Vigne (2001) for looking at burglary.

38 Burgess, E. W. (1928). Factors determining success or failure on parole. In A. A. Bruce, E. W. Burgess, & A. J. Harno (Eds.), *The Workings of the Indeterminate Sentence Law and the Parole System in Illinois* (pp. 221-234). Springfield: Illinois State Board of Parole; Glueck, S. & Glueck, E. (1950). *Unraveling juvenile delinquence*. New York: Commonwealth; Miller, J. & Lin, J. (2007). Applying a generic juvenile risk assessment instrument to a local context: Some practical and theoretical lessons. *Crime and Delinquency, 53*, 552-580.

39 Gottfredson, S. D. & Moriarty, L. J. (2006). Statistical risk assessment: Old problems and new applications. *Crime and Delinquency, 52*, 178-200.

40 Marczyk, G. R., Heilbrun, K., Lander, T., & DeMatteo, D. S. (2003). Prediction juvenile recidivism with the PCL-YV, MAYSI, and YLS-CMI. *International Journal of Forensic Mental Health, 2*, 7-18; Wiebush, R. G., Baird, C., Krisberg, B., & Onek, D. (1995). Risk assessment and classification for serious, violent, and chronic juvenile offenders. In J. C. Howell, B. Krisberg, J. D. Hawkins, & J. J. Wilson (Eds), *A sourcebook: Serious, violent, & chronic juvenile offenders* (pp. 171-210). Thousand Oaks, CA: Sage.

41 Ratcliffe, J. H. & McCullagh, M. J. (2001). Chasing ghosts? Police perception of high crime areas. *British Journal of Criminology, 41*: 330-341.

42 Caplan, J. M., & Kennedy, L. (2009, February). *Drug arrests, shootings, and gang residences in Irvington, NJ: An exercise in data discovery*. Paper presented at Threat Assessments: Innovations and Applications in Data Integration and Analysis Conference at the Regional Operations Intelligence Center, West Trenton, NJ.

43 Cohen, L. E. & Felson, M. (1979). Social change and crime rate trends: A routine activity approach. *American Sociological Review, 44*: 588-608.

44 For example: Braga, A. (2005). Hot spots policing and crime prevention: A systematic review of randomized controlled trials. Journal of Experimental Criminology. 1: 317-342; Sherman, L. W, Gartin, P. R. & Buerger, M. E. (1989). Hot spots of predatory crime: Routine activities and the criminology of place. Criminology. 27: 821-849.

45 Groff, E. R. & La Vigne, N. G. (2001). Mapping an opportunity surface of residential burglary. *Journal of Research in Crime and Delinquency. 38*: 257-278; Groff, E. R. & La Vigne, N.G. (2002). Forecasting the future of predictive crime mapping. *Crime Prevention Studies. 13*: 29-57.

46 Johnson, S., Birks, D. J., McLaughlin, L., Bowers, K. J., & Pease, K. (2007). Prospective Crime Mapping in Operational Context, Home Office, London; Kennedy, L. W. & Van Brunschot, E. G. (2009). *The Risk in Crime*. New York: Roman and Littlefield.

47 Brantingham, P. and P. Brantingham. 1995. "Criminality of Place: Crime Generators and Crime Attractors." European Journal on Criminal Policy and Research 3:1-26.

48 Berk, R. (2009). *Asymmetric loss functions for forecasting in criminal justice settings.* [unpublished manuscript]; Chainey, S., Tompson, L., & Uhlig, S. (2008). The utility of hotspot mapping for predicting spatial patterns of crime. *Security Journal. 21*: 4-28.

49 Johnson, S., Birks, D. J., McLaughlin, L., Bowers, K. J., & Pease, K. (2007). Prospective Crime Mapping in Operational Context, Home Office, London.

[50] Gorr, W. & Olligschlaeger, A. (2002). Crime Hot Spot Forecasting: Modeling and Comparative Evaluation, National Institute of Justice, Washington, DC.

[51] Groff, E. R. & La Vigne, N. G. (2001). Mapping an opportunity surface of residential burglary. *Journal of Research in Crime and Delinquency*. 38: 257-278.

[52] For example, see: Gorr, W. & Olligschlaeger, A. (2002). Crime Hot Spot Forecasting: Modeling and Comparative Evaluation, National Institute of Justice, Washington, DC; Berk, R. (2009). *Asymmetric loss functions for forecasting in criminal justice settings.* [unpublished manuscript].

[53] Johnson, S., Birks, D. J., McLaughlin, L., Bowers, K. J., & Pease, K. (2007). Prospective Crime Mapping in Operational Context, Home Office, London.

[54] http://www.npr.org/blogs/alltechconsidered/2010/05/24/127088641/the-path-from-syphilis-to-faster-mris

[55] http://www.npr.org/blogs/alltechconsidered/2010/05/24/127088641/the-path-from-syphilis-to-faster-mris

[56] Fagan, J. A. & Wilkinson, D. L. (1998). Guns, youth violence, and social identity in inner cities. In Toney, M. & Moore, M. (eds.), Crime and Justice: Annual Review of Research (Vol. 24), University of Chicago Press, Chicago, pp. 105-188; Brantingham, P. J., & Brantingham, P. L. (1981). *Environmental Criminology*. Sage. Beverly Hills; Klein, M. (1995). *The American Street Gang*, Oxford University Press, London.

[57] Brantingham, P. & Brantingham, P. 1995. "Criminality of Place: Crime Generators and Crime Attractors." *European Journal on Criminal Policy and Research* 3:1-26; Roncek, D. W., & Maier, P. A. (1991). Bars, blocks and crimes revisited: Linking the theory of routine activities to the empiricism of "hot spots." *Criminology*. 29: 725-753.

[58] Lum, C. (2008). The geography of drug activity and violence: Analyzing spatial relationships of non-homogenous crime event types. *Substance Use & Misuse*. 43: 179-201; Blumstein, A. (1995). Youth violence, guns, and the illicit-drug industry. *Journal of Criminal Law and Criminology*. 86: 10-36.

[59] Felson, M. (1995). Those who discourage crime. In J.E. Eck & D. Weisburd (eds.), Crime *and Place: Crime Prevention Studies. Vol. 4.* Washington, D.C.: Police Executive Research Forum; Taylor, R. B. (1997). Social order and disorder of street-blocks and neighborhood: Ecology, microecology and the systemic model of social disorganization. *Journal of Research in Crime and Delinquency 24*, 113-155; Taylor, R. B. & Harrell, A. V. (1996). *Physical Environment and Crime*. Washington, D.C.: National Institute of Justice.

[60] Ratcliffe, J. H. & McCullagh, M. J. (2001). Chasing ghosts? Police perception of high crime areas. *British Journal of Criminology, 41*: 330-341.

[61] Ratcliffe, J. H. & Rengert, G. F. (2008). Near repeat patterns in Philadelphia shootings, *Security Journal*, 21(1-2): 58-76.

[62] To learn more about analyzing data with Microsoft Excel, see *Better policing with Microsoft Office: Crime analysis, investigations and community policing* by Stallo and Bruce.

[63] Caplan, J. M., Kennedy, L. W., & Miller, J. (2010, online); Kennedy, L. W., Caplan, J. M., & Piza, E. (n.d.)

[64] Anselin, L., Cohen, J., Cook, D., Gorr, W. & Tita, G., (2000). Spatial analyses of crime. In Duffee, D. (ed.), Measurement and Analysis of Crime and Justice: Criminal Justice 2000 (Vol. 4), National Institute of Justice, Washington, DC, pp. 213-262.

[65] Anselin, L. (2003). *GeoDa 0.9 user's guide, spatial analysis laboratory.* Urbana-Champaign: University of Illinois. http://geodacenter.org/downloads/pdfs/geoda093.pdf

[66] Ratcliffe, J. H. & McCullagh, M. J. (2001). Chasing ghosts? Police perception of high crime areas. *British Journal of Criminology, 41*: 330-341.

[67] Kennedy, L. W. & Van Brunschot, E. G. (2009). *The Risk in Crime*. New York: Roman and Littlefield.

[68] For example, see: Sampson, R.J., S.W. Raudenbush, and F. Earls 1997 Neighborhoods and Violent Crime: A Multilevel Study of Collective Efficacy Science 277, 15: 918-924.

Made in the USA
Lexington, KY
12 October 2011